AUTHOR	CLASS No.
HUNTER, R.H.	940·5421
TITLE	BOOK No.
Battle coast	450004155

D0101843

THE D-DAY ASSAULT

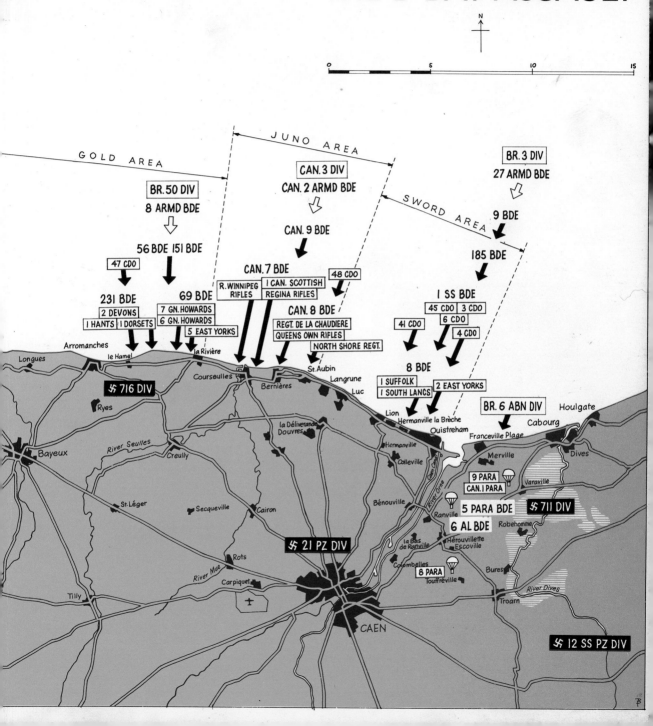

BATTLE COAST

BATTLE COAST

by
R. H. HUNTER & T. H. C. BROWN

An Illustrated History of D-Day
The Sixth of June
1944

SPURBOOKS LIMITED

The Battle Coast
first published by
SPURBOOKS LTD
1 STATION ROAD
BOURNE END
BUCKINGHAMSHIRE
ENGLAND

450004155

© T. H. C. BROWN, R. H. HUNTER 1973

SBN 0 902875 24 8

Printed in Great Britain by
Biddles Ltd., Guildford, Surrey.

CONTENTS

AUTHOR'S FOREWORD

Many books have been written about D-Day, so why another one? The main reason is that the story itself is still fascinating, while the battlefield can still be visited, and the one related to the other.

Moreover, after a certain lapse of time, it is possible to get a battle into perspective, and decide, even if only for oneself, was it decisive, a disaster, a waste of time and lives?

In writing and illustrating this book we have had to do an immense amount of reading, researching, talking, listening, and travelling — for the story is like a ball of wool, constantly tangled, constantly unravelling. For every incident included, ten have had to be omitted. The selections are arbitrary, and of our own choice, and no slight is intended to persons or units omitted from this history. It is only our book, it was their battle. We hope we have caught the flavour of the time, and told, in simple terms, the story of the greatest invasion in the history of the world. The chapter quotes, inevitably, are from Henry V — what else?

R. H. Hunter
T. H. C. Brown
London, 1973

This book is dedicated to
The Commando Units
of
The Royal Marines

1940-1944

Into a thousand parts divide one man
And make imaginary puissance . . .

Carry them here and there; jumping o'er times;
Turning the accomplishment of many years
Into an hourglass.

This is a history of D-Day, a guide to the events and places of the battlefield, and to the people, problems and solutions that made the D-Day landings possible.

It is, therefore, about a place, a plan, and millions of people, English, German, American, French, Canadian, Polish — a whole world of people.

To tell such a story in simple terms is difficult, because of the very size and scale of the D-Day operation, because a major operation of war is inevitably complicated, and because, of all such operations, an invasion is the most complicated of all, and D-Day was, and will happily remain, the biggest amphibious operation in history.

To the story, and this book, this is however an advantage, for in the complication of the enterprise lies half the fascination of the story. Moreover one can now illustrate the text with a selection from the thousands of photographs now available, and unravel at least some of the technicalities with line drawings and maps.

Every story must have a beginning, and the story of 'Operation Overlord', the Allied

Invasion of Europe, on 6th June, 1944, really began on the night of the 4th June, 1940, when a destroyer sailed from Dunkirk with the last of the British Expeditionary Force. There would be a long and painful gap of four years before another British Army set foot again in France.

When Hitler decided to halt his Armies' advance in the West, thus allowing the British to make good their escape, although without most of their arms and equipment, his decision was as puzzling to his opponents as it was frustrating to his Generals. Neither side could see the sense in it.

Nevertheless, Hitler had his reasons, and they were, to him anyway, perfectly valid. He had served in the trenches during the stalemate of the Great War, and studied the strategic doctrines of Molke and Schiefflen in the years since. He had his enemies on the run, and must avoid, as the Great War Generals had not, any diversion in the West that might permit entrenchment, and a return to static warfare. His Blitzkrieg tactics had put victory within his grasp, and he had only to seize it.

British forces withdraw through Dunkirk, June 1940.

11

The beaches of Dunkirk, June 1940.

To do this, the Wehrmacht had to keep moving on to the capture of the political prize, Paris, and ignore the military satisfaction of rounding up the shattered British on the Channel Coast.

If Paris fell, the defeat of France and the domination of Europe were assured, and if the price of this was to let the English escape back to their island, it was a price that Hitler was very willing to pay.

The Fuehrer was sure, anyway, that, whatever happened, Britain was out of the war. He would, if possible, reach some accommodation with the British in the West, as he had done with the Russians in the East before the outbreak of war. If he could not make peace with the British, then his U-Boats would see that they starved, and his Luftwaffe would pound them into submission. He had viewed the British at Munich, and had his own opinion of them as a nation. 'They are worms', he stated.

Hitler's view of the British and their leaders had been formed during the years of

Spitfires scramble.

appeasement, and he can hardly be blamed for acquiring such opinions. He had not, at this time, heard of the old English proverb that even a worm can turn.

Even if he had, the military might of Britain had been dissipated in the debacle of Dunkirk, as, although most of the troops got back to England, most of their weapons and equipment had been left behind. In the Second War, as in the First, the strength of Britain rested primarily in the short term, on the Royal Navy, and in the long term, on what strength she could muster in the Empire. The British have an irritating habit of not being able to see the writing on the wall, until their backs are pressed against it. At such times, when a sensible people would be steeped in worry and despair the British become cheerful.

Certainly the mood of the country after the capitulation of France was almost gay, people were friendly and talked to one another in public places in a most un-British way, and speculated aloud and at length on how long it would take to beat the Germans this time.

What exactly they were to beat them with was the problem.

The only bright spot for the British on the military front in mid-June 1940 was that at least a drawn out trench struggle had been avoided. This in turn meant that to free Europe from Hitler, the English must invade Europe. But that problem, it was generally recognised, was a long way off in 1940. More immediate was the prospect of the Germans invading England, where no doubt the British could give them a long overdue hiding.

In June 1940, the defence of the free world depended on 25 miles of the English Channel, and 1,243 men, the trained fighter pilots of the Royal Air Force. In 1803 Admiral St. Vincent had been asked in Parliament if Napoleon's Army, then poised near Bologne, could invade England. His Lordship gave a typically English answer. 'I do not say they cannot come', he said carefully. 'I only say they cannot come by sea.'

The Admiral had made a neat point and Europe smiled at it. His ironic pride and faith in the Royal Navy to keep the Narrow Seas, was still strong in the hearts of the English 137 years later, but the situation was now more complicated.

The British Navy could certainly destroy any German invasion fleet. Unfortunately, the bombers of the German Luftwaffe could destroy the Royal Navy. However, to do that, the Luftwaffe had first to destroy the fighters of the Royal Air Force, and gain air superiority over the Channel, as they had already over Poland, France and the Low Countries. This, as one can see, makes a rather deadly pecking order, in which, with his larger and more experienced fighter arm, equipped in the main with superior machines, the advantage lay with the Germans. They should, at the odds, drive the R.A.F. from the skies, and gain for the invader the first requirement for his task, air superiority.

In June 1940 it hadn't come to that. Not yet. First Hitler tried peace offers and blandishments. When these failed he tried threats. Only when the British still refused to negotiate, did he revert to type. Force was always his ultimate persuader.

'As England, in spite of her hopeless military position, has shown herself unwilling to come to any compromise I have decided to begin preparations for, and if necessary to carry out, the invasion of England . . .

'The English Airforce must be eliminated to such an extent that it will be incapable of putting up any substantial opposition to the invading troops'.

All military operations of any size have code names, and Hitler's invasion was code-named 'OPERATION SEA-LION'.

The story of the Battle of Britain, the defeat of the Luftwaffe, and the abandonment of SEA-LION belong elsewhere, and we must press on with our story. But a lesson was found to be a fact and the relevant facts in 1940 still held good in 1944. The first requirement for a successful cross Channel invasion was control of the air.

If Hitler could not invade England, and finish the war, it followed that one day the British and their Allies must go back to France and settle the issue there. The road back would be a long one, but the first step had already been taken. On 22nd June, two weeks after Dunkirk, a party of British

British Commando, German M.G. 34 machine gun.

Commandos made a reconnaisance raid near Bologne.

The raid achieved very little, but it was the start of a long series of amphibious landings, large and small, that would develop amphibious operational techniques to a high state of expertise, and gain for the Allies a mass of knowledge about the defences of the enemy coast. These were two more of the invasion requirements, skill in amphibious techniques and knowledge of the enemy defences.

To the achievement of both these objectives, the Commandos were created, small units, the men trained to act like packs of hounds, until in the words of their creator, 'There shall come a steel hand from the sea, to pluck the enemy's sentries from their posts.'

The creator was the Prime Minister, Winston Churchill, and the raising of the Commandos illustrates the ability of the British to react to the requirements of a difficult situation, and to learn, even from an enemy.

The Commando Memorial at Spean Bridge, Scotland.

In South Africa, 40 years before, a Boer Commando had destroyed a train in which Churchill was travelling and captured him. In 1940, because the situation required it, he recreated light raiding forces, and called them after his old adversaries.

It is strange, but true, that the British in war have a reputation for being, in their thinking and in the execution of their plans, slow, ponderous, over cautious and reactionary. That this reputation is at odds with the facts is obvious when one considers that in World War II alone, no nation produced, planned or implemented more original military ideas than the British.

The Commandos, the Special Operations Executive, the Special Air Service Regiments, Combined Operations H.Q., Mulberry Harbours, specialised armour, and a host of other ingenious formations or devices all came from or were developed to significance by, not the inventive Americans, or technically minded Germans, but the supposedly dull and plodding British. A national tolerance of eccentrics has certain advantages.

Churchill set up a Combined Operations Headquarters in July 1940 to raise special units, to harass the enemy, and to plan for the invasion of Europe.

In the next few years, the Commandos gained in experience and reputation, making major raids on Lofoton and Vaagso in Norway, at St. Nazaire in France, and in hundreds of smaller raids along the coast of Hitler's 'Fortress Europe'.

Meanwhile, the war moved on. The Germans and Italians invaded Greece, and drove out the British. A further set-back followed in Crete, where the German paratroops made their only significant air-

Territory occupied by the AXIS in 1944.

16

The convoys bring war material to Britain.

borne operation of the war, at grievous cost to themselves, indicating another invasion lesson, that lightly equipped paratroops must receive quick relief to avoid destruction and air support to survive at all.

In the Western Desert, the war flowed to and fro along the coast, as first one side, then the other, gained the upper hand.

1941 appeared in many respects the black year for the freedom cause, but it was in the end the year in which the Germans reached the peak of their power and from then on the path was, however imperceptibly, on the downward course to ruin, for in 1941 the Axis overreached themselves.

On 2nd June, violating the neutrality pact which had enabled him to rape Western Europe with impunity, Hitler invaded Russia, and drove the Red Armies before him in defeat.

Six months later on 7th December, Hitler's other allies, the Japanese, attacked the American Pacific Fleet at Pearl Harbour and the United States entered the war.

Both these steps brought the invasion of Europe perceptibly nearer.

For a start, allied first to Britain and later to the U.S.A. as well, Russia began to scream loudly for help. In this the Russian government, whose alliance and non-aggression pact with Hitler had paved the way for Hitler's triumphs in 1939 and 1940, displayed considerable gall. The situation in which they found themselves was largely of their own making and Russia was now simply receiving, at German hands, treatment she had been happy to see meted out to others, people she now demanded come at once to her assistance.

However strong the temptation to rub Russia's nose in the origins of her own predicament, the temptation was generally resisted and Allied aid flowed to Russia in powerful convoys that fought Arctic seas, submarines and bombers to take Russia the weapons of war, with scant assistance from the Russians themselves.

Russia's principal demand was for the immediate opening of a Second Front in the West, to take the Germans in the rear, and take the pressure off the homeland, and when the United States entered the war, urgent consideration was given by the Allies to the Russian demand.

On 20th December 1941, two weeks after Pearl Harbour, Winston Churchill and the American President, Franklin D. Roosevelt met in Washington and held what became known as the Arcadia Conference. During this conference two decisions were arrived at that proved instrumental in developing plans for the invasion of Europe.

The first was the setting up of a unified Allied Command, the Combined Chiefs of Staff, to jointly direct the Anglo-American war effort. This was done in the light of the bitter experience of the Great War when the British and French fought under separate commands until near defeat in March 1918 finally united them under Foch. In this war there was to be unity from the beginning and although not without strain, this unity managed to hold firm to the end.

The second major decision was the 'Germany First' policy. It was decided that the Allied effort be directed first and foremost to the defeat of Germany and American Armies were to go into action against the Germans as soon as possible.

The decision was based upon the classic, well established article of strategic doctrine which states that when faced with an array of enemies, the strongest should be defeated first. Although strategically sound and mutually agreed, the Americans had some misgivings about how far the Allies could go in excluding the Japanese in the Pacific from their calculations. In particular, Admiral King, Commander-in-Chief of the United States Navy, agreed to the 'Germany First' policy only with the greatest reluctance.

The American Pacific Fleet had suffered a major and infamous attack at Pearl Harbour, and Admiral King wanted to hit back. Moreover he did not see how the Japanese could ever be defeated if they were given years to consolidate their conquests in the Pacific, and assurances of total effort from the British and American Commands in the Pacific, immediately Germany was defeated, failed to reassure him.

Also, the Pacific would be primarily a Naval theatre of operations where Admiral King's command would dominate Allied strategy, and he had no objection to that.

Finally Admiral King disliked the British in general and the Royal Navy in particular.

In the event, Admiral King with MacArthur and that magnificent fighting force, the United States Marines, fought on in the Pacific in an island hopping campaign that turned the tide of Japanese victory into defeat, but his attitude to the European theatre and the British did have one unfortunate effect on the European theatre, and on the OVERLORD operation, for King controlled the allocation to theatres of the ships produced in the American shipyards. As a result of this, the Allied cause in Europe and the Mediterranean suffered from a chronic shortage of landing craft and support vessels from 1942 until the end of the war.

American agreement to the 'Germany First' policy was on the understanding that the war was carried across the English Channel into Europe as quickly as possible.

The Americans first intention was to build up an army in England and then strike across the Channel into France.

Roosevelt and his advisers proposed to reach this stage in the summer of 1942, six months after entering the war. At this time the American Armies had not met the Wehrmacht.

The British, somewhat to America's annoyance, were more than a little dubious about the success of such a venture and said so in unmistakeable terms until, as American troops began to land in Britain in mid 1942, a stream of high-ranking American politicians and military men also began to arrive in London to urge the British into action. The Russians were loudly demanding a Second Front and General Marshall, the American Army Chief of Staff, conscious of the need to support Russia, proposed that the Allies might cross the Channel in the autumn of 1942 to establish a small bridgehead, perhaps in the Cherbourg Peninsula, which they would maintain via the port of Cherbourg throughout the winter, and from which they would charge out in the spring and win the war. This operation bore the code name 'SLEDGE-HAMMER'.

Exactly what the Germans would be doing about this situation during the winter of 1942-43 was not discussed.

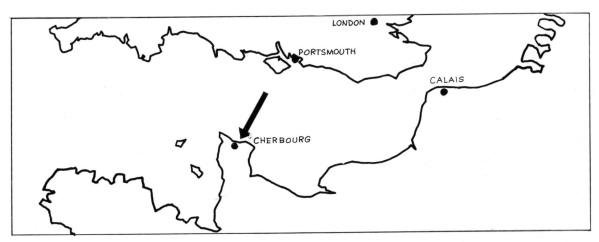

"Sledgehammer" operation plan for 1943.

Submarine depth-charged in the North Atlantic.

Whatever the tactical merits of the plan, strategic considerations alone made it a non-starter. The Battle of the Atlantic, the war against the U-boat, was being bitterly fought and the U-boat was, at this stage anyway, savaging the convoys and thus restricting the build up of Allied strength in Britain. The British had a major commitment to defeat General Rommel's Afrika Corps in the Western desert, and finally the Luftwaffe were holding their own in the skies of France and the Allied air offensive against Germany had still to develop.

The impossibility of 'SLEDGEHAMMER' was bloodily underlined in August 1942 when the 2nd Canadian Division and three British Commandos, with naval and air support, attempted a coup-de-main against the French Port of Dieppe.

A strong sense of scepticism is useful in the study of military affairs, especially when it comes to accepting the reasons given for a certain course of action, for different reasons tend to appear depending on whether the operation succeeded or not.

The Dieppe raid has been described as a reconnaissance in force and Lord Mountbatten, who was Chief of Combined Operations, has stated that even as the Battle of Waterloo was won on the playing fields of Eton, so the Battle of D-Day was won on the beaches of Dieppe, and there is a lot of truth in that assertion.

The Dieppe raid taught the Allies a lesson. It was however, a lesson they probably knew already and the question remains, what, had Dieppe been taken, did the Allies intend to do with it. Itself a failure, Dieppe was a further development of the knowledge necessary for a successful invasion. To understand the lessons of Dieppe requires some knowledge of

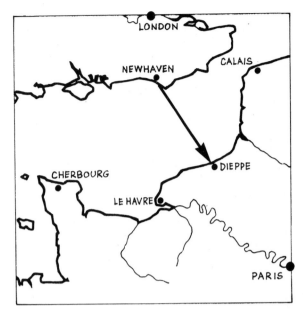

The South of England and the invasion coast of France.

logistics, that branch of the military art concerned with supply.

Without supplies, petrol, food, ammunition, medical supplies and men, armies cannot function for long. For any army the problem is considerable, but for an invading army, the basic problem of delivering the right things in the right amount, to the right unit at the right time is compounded by the physical problem of getting them ashore, in all weathers and probably against a variety of opposition. This physical problem is of course greatly eased if a proper functioning port is available.

Needless to say, the enemy is equally aware of this, and sees to it that all ports are well defended and if in danger of capture, extensively destroyed and made unusable.

For the invasion to have had a chance of success the Allies would need a port in good working order, through which the army ashore could be supplied, safe from interruption by winter gales. And so Dieppe. The big question to be answered was, is it possible to capture a port by assault, before the enemy have time to make it unusable? It wasn't.

The cost of demonstrating the impossibility of taking a port was expensive. Of the 5,000 Canadians who set out, 3,300 were killed, wounded or captured. Their tanks never got off the beach, coastal defences were not knocked out, and the Luftwaffe appeared in abundance. The Raid did, luckily lead to a number of innovations in the amphibious equipment of the Allies and in the tactical deployment of troops in the assault role.

The biggest innovation, having accepted that to seize a port was impossible, was that the invading army must take a floating port with them, and the designing of what were to be the 'Mulberry' harbours commenced. The slaughter of infantry on the beaches led to the employment of tanks in the initial assault waves and the inability of the standard tank to cope with beach conditions and obstacles led directly to the development of specialized armour.

Although Dieppe was a not unexpected defeat, the war took a turn for the better two months later, when the British Eighth Army, under General Montgomery, attacked Rommel's Afrika Corps at El Alamain and after heavy fighting drove them back on the road to final defeat in North Africa.

In December, the Americans went into action in North Africa, when they landed in Rommel's rear, under the command of Major-General Dwight D. Eisenhower.

The three future protagonists of D-Day, Rommel, Montgomery and Eisenhower, met here in battle for the first time.

The North African campaign dragged on until the late spring of 1943, thus effectively ruling out a cross Channel invasion in that year. By the time the Afrika Corps were eliminated, there was no time left to reorganise and switch the landing craft Allied strength to Western Europe.

Instead, Sicily was invaded, Italy driven out of the war, and most significantly for the Cross-Channel invasion, the U-boat menace finally controlled if not defeated, in the Battle of the Atlantic. With the decline of the U-boat, the Naval strength necessary for the invasion could begin to gather.

About this time, the invasion acquired a code name. They called it 'OPERATION OVERLORD'.

From the beginning there had been agreement that the Supreme Commander of OVERLORD would be an American for after the initial landing, the bulk of the ground forces would be American, and for this if for no other reason, the appointment of an American as 'Supreme Commander, Allied Expeditionary Force', was inevitable.

It was also becoming apparent in 1943, that whatever the fate of the Axis Powers, the war would see the eclipse of Britain as a Great Power, and that OVERLORD would be the final great effort of a nation economically nearing exhaution.

This too was inevitable, for twice in thirty years, Britain had been bled white in two World Wars defending democracy while American made up her mind. In addition, during 1943 the American Government were commencing a love affair with Russia, that lasted until the closing of the Berlin Corridor in 1947 finally forced the Americans to recognise the people they were dealing with.

In 1943 the Americans felt themselves to

have more in common with the Russians than with the imperialistic British, and bluntly pointed out to Churchill that the American people were not pouring out blood and treasure to free the world from fascism only to return the freed nations of the world to their former colonial masters. This attitude applied particularly to the British, and sounded very high-minded, but there was in addition, some cold logic behind it.

Roosevelt may very well have detested colonialism, however benign, but his reasons for seeking rapid self determination for the colonies of Britain, France and the Netherlands were not unmixed altruism.

He had been elected in the middle of the American depression, and seen America return to prosperity on a tide of war work. He had no intention of seeing these gains disappear after the peace, with the run down of an industry geared to war production.

To insure against this he needed large export markets. Some would come from the rebuilding of war-torn Europe, and the British Empire could supply the rest, if old political and economic ties could be broken.

Roosevelt began working to this end before America entered the war, and the Lease Land Act, which supplied Britain with war material, included clauses aimed at the abolition of Imperial preference, the basis of Empire trade, thus giving America free access to traditional British markets.

Added to Roosevelt's determination to open up the Empire, was his conviction that he could handle Stalin. He believed that by making clear his detestation of colonialism, and by mocking Churchill in Stalin's presence, he could win the Russian support to the Anglo-American side. To be fair he warned Churchill that he was going to try such a

Franklin D. Roosevelt, President of the United States.

tactic, but Stalin probably regarded this as sheer weakness, and he took every opportunity from then on to play an ally off against the other, especially in pouring cold water on the British plans for the war in Italy, and campaigns in the Balkans.

He was, in any event, glad to see the British unsupported in the high commands of the war, for the British were having increasing doubts about Russia's long term political ambitions during and after the war, particularly in Eastern Europe and the Balkans.

23

Winston Churchill inspects bomb-damage in London.

Churchill made no secret of the fact that the further East the Red Army were kept the better it would be for the future peace of Europe, for he in his turn, saw no future in freeing Europe from the Nazis if it was then to be dominated by the Communists. Roosevelt put Churchill's views on the Russians down to his inbred imperialism, and although time has proved Churchill right, he was at the time, powerless to prevent Russian influence expanding, with tacit American consent.

With these and other political strains tugging at the Alliance, the Anglo-Americans were fortunate in the man chosen to lead them in OVERLORD.

General Eisenhower was, by any standards, a good soldier, a fine man, and unequalled as a leader of disparate Allied armies. He could handle prickly army Commanders tactfully or slap them down hard if he saw the need to, without lasting rancour, for he was universally liked and respected and his smile alone was reputedly worth an army corps to the Allied

General Dwight D. Eisenhower.

cause. Commanding a vast force from many nations, Eisenhower himself was entirely without nationalistic prejudice, but he tolerated it in others, and his staff, following his example, worked together in an atmosphere remarkably free from national friction. For internal disagreements among his staff, Eisenhower's rule was simple. 'If you disagree strongly with someone you can call him a bastard if you have to. You may not, however, call him a Limey or a Yankee bastard.'

The Allies would need a lot of luck to get ashore in Europe, but their first and biggest piece of luck was in the appointment of Eisenhower as Commanding General.

Before commanding in North Africa, Eisenhower had never had an operational command. He was by profession a staff officer, of considerable experience, and a protegee of General Marshall, the American Army Chief of Staff.

This gave Eisenhower considerable political influence, and knowledge of how to get his views across to people in a position to help, and this, added to his universal popularity, made him the perfect man for the job.

Eisenhower's appointment as Supreme Commander was confirmed on Christmas Day 1943 when he was still in North Africa.

The Senior Command structure for OVERLORD was as follows:

Organisation — S.H.A.E.F.

Supreme Commander:
General Eisenhower (U.S.)

Deputy Supreme Commander:
Air Chief Marshal Tedder (U.K.)

Chief of Staff:
General Bedell Smith (U.S.)

| C-in-C Allied Naval Forces: | C-in-C Allied Air Forces: |
| Admiral Bertram Ramsey (U.K.) | Air Chief Marshal Leigh Mallory (U.K.) |

Commander — Ground Forces:
General Sir Bernard L. Montgomery

General Montgomery.

These were the tactical Air and Naval forces allocated for the invasion. The strategic Naval and Air Forces had separate tasks and were not at this time controlled directly by Eisenhower.

The Army field commander for the invasion and build up period was the British General Montgomery, commanding what became known as the 21st Army Group, which included all land forces, British, Canadian and American, during the landing, it being understood that he would revert to Commander 21st Army Group, which would then consist solely of British and Canadian forces, when sufficient American troops were ashore to form a separate Army Group under General Omar Bradley, at which time General Eisenhower would assume overall tactical control of the Allied Armies in Europe. Eisenhower's command was known as S.H.A.E.F., (Supreme Headquarters Allied Expeditionary Force). Meanwhile, during the

S.H.A.E.F. Standing left to right: *Lt. Gen. Omar Bradley, Admiral Ramsay, Air Marshal Trafford Leigh Mallory, Lt. Gen. Bedell-Smith.* Seated left to right: *Air Chief Marshal Tedder, Gen. Eisenhower, Gen. Montgomery.*

landings, General Bradley would command the American 1st Army.

One New Year's Eve, at Marrakech in Morocco, Eisenhower and Montgomery had their first look at plans already prepared for OVERLORD.

This plan had been in preparation since 1942, and was the work of a planning team under the direction of Lt. General Morgan. His appointment was entitled 'Chief of Staff to the Supreme Allied Commander (Designate)' or COSSAC for short, and the plan was therefore known as the COSSAC plan.

The war had, as already described, laid down the requirements necessary for a successful invasion and as more requirements became evident, so they were incorporated in the plan. The basic requirements were straightforward.

The ground invasion area must be within reach of Allied air cover; provide weather-protected landing beaches; permit rapid deployment of the Allied armies after the

U.S. Troops train in Britain 1943.

U.S. Troops feeding the pigeons in Trafalgar Square 1943.

invasion; be capable of sealing off by bombing communications, to delay the building up of enemy counter offensives and have some reasonable port facility that could quickly be cleared of mines and obstructions and brought into use.

For the first requirement the Channel coast around Calais would be best as it was a bare twenty minutes flying time away from the airfields in Kent. It was so suitable that the enemy agreed with the Allies and their assessment, and their defences as at Dieppe, were considered too strong for a successful assault. To the north the landing area was more suitable but a break-out would lead across the flood plain of Flanders, and this tended to eliminate this area as the Germans could convert this area into a swamp and bog the advancing Allies down.

Further north still, the coast was open to the strong waves of the North Sea, so the COSSAC planners turned their eyes south.

The coast of Normandy, and in particular the area between the Cotentin peninsula and the Bay of the Seine lay only 80 miles away from the South Coast of England, just in fighter range. The beaches were wide and shallow and the Cotentin peninsula, apart from offering the port of Cherbourg gave some protection from the full fetch of the Atlantic gales. Moreover the area could be cut off by tactical bombing of some 30 bridges leading across the Seine to the East, thus isolating the area from German reinforcement. Finally in this sector, the coastal fortifications were nowhere near as strong as they were along the Channel coast. COSSAC chose Normandy for the OVERLORD invasion.

Eisenhower and Montgomery had many reservations about the COSSAC plan, and with the invasion date given as 1st May 1944 only a few months to do much about it. They did, however, agree that the choice of a landing place was correct and thus the die was cast.

Sometime soon, in the coming year the weight of Allied arms would fall on Normandy.

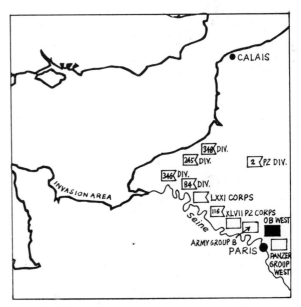

German forces north of the Seine, contained there by aerial interdiction.

THE DEFENCES OF NORMANDY

'Thus come the English with full power upon us
And more than carefully it us concerns . . .
To line and new repair our towns of war
With men of courage and with means defendent'.

Normandy, ancient dukedom of the English Kings is the largest province in modern France. As with all French provinces it is sub-divided into a number of Departments, of which two, Calvados and La Manche, were to be directly concerned with the invasion on their northern and eastern coasts. Both departments are agricultural, given over to arable farming, the growing of cider apples, horse breeding and, in the summer, some small scale tourism.

The Calvados coast runs west, from the mouth of the River Orne at Ouistreham to the mouth of the River Vire, north of Isigny. Before the War it was a holiday and tourist area, noted for fine safe beaches, yachting and abundant and excellent sea food. The coast near Ouistreham, running through the little towns of Lion sur Mer, Luc sur Mer, Langrune and St. Aubin is referred to locally as 'Le Côte Nacre', The Pearl Coast.

Across the Vire, in the west, one enters the Department of La Manche, which stretches west through Carentan and north up the Cotentin Peninsula through the beautiful little town of Ste-Mere-Eglise to Cherbourg, the major port in this section of the coast and the nearest port to Southern England.

The beaches everywhere are very wide, flat and sandy, gently shelving and backed either with drained salt marshes or low sand-dunes. In the west, north of Isigny the area is sparsely developed except for a few farms and small hamlets and only in the east along the 'Côte Nacre', are there any towns fronting directly onto the sea. Across the sea wall are the wide shelving sandy beaches, typical of the region.

The beaches are broken only once, in the section between the Vire and Arromanches where steep cliffs 100 feet high drop directly into the sea along 20 miles of coast. These cliffs in turn, are broken only twice, by the small harbour and town of Port-en-Bassin, and by four miles of beach at Vierville. This beach was code named OMAHA.

The country behind the beaches is very varied, with large open areas of arable fields being interspersed with orchards, low wooded hills, and the close irregular fields of the Normandy bocage. Bocage is a Norman word, meaning grove or copse. The Normandy

Coastal defences in Normandy.

31

Heavy guns overlooked the harbour at Port en Bessin.

A long range German gun in a concrete emplacement.

bocage consisted of innumerable small irregular fields divided by thick hedges set atop earth banks, two to three feet high. This was perfect defensive country if the enemy had time and forces to occupy it. Overall the country is not unlike Hampshire, or the flatter areas of Vermont and Maine in the Eastern United States.

The coast offered few natural advantages or disadvantages to invader or defender, other than some low lying marsh land around Carentan and a number of slow, narrow, winding rivers, but inland the bocage was to be of great assistance to the Germans.

Communications along the coast are dependent on an adequate road network, with main road junctions at St. Lô in the west and Caen in the east. A study of the end paper maps reveals, even to the layman, the importance of swiftly capturing Caen, St. Lô, Carentan and Ste-Mere-Eglise.

In the centre of the Calvados strip some ten miles inland from the coast, lies the ancient cathedral city of Bayeux, famous down the ages for that remarkable relic of another invasion, Bishop Odo's Bayeux Tapestry, which records the landing of Duke William in England nine centuries ago.

There are no other towns of any size near the coast, with the exceptions of the port of Ouistreham at the mouth of the Orne, population about 5,000, Carentan, population also 5,000, at the base of the Cotentin, and Ste-Mere-Eglise, population 1,400, all of which are market centres for the surrounding countryside, but of no real size.

Taken all together, Normandy was a backwater in the European war, quiet, peaceful and relatively undisturbed, and had remained such since German forces over-ran France in 1940. It was occupied by second rate formations with obsolescent equipment, or by divisions resting after campaigns on the Russian Front.

The options open to generals are always limited, and simply by calculating what they would do in Eisenhower's place, the Germans were able to predict when and where the invasion would probably come.

The choice clearly lay between the Pas de Calais, favoured by Von Rundstedt, the German Commander in the West, and most of the German High Command, the OKW, and Normandy, favoured on intuitive reasons, by Hitler. Both parties felt that whichever part the main invasion came in, there would be a major diversion in the other, to disperse the defenders and help the main assault.

The difficulty would be to decide which was the invasion and which the diversion.

Hitler possessed, throughout the war, an almost uncanny ability to predict the time and place of enemy attacks. Although there was dispute between his generals and himself about the location of the invasion, and when it would come, there was no doubt that it would come, almost certainly in the Spring or early Summer of 1944. He had therefore some six months to prepare for it, and there was much to be done. He did, however, have just the man to do it.

Field Marshal Erwin Rommel, infantry colonel, panzer leader, sometime leader of the doughty Afrika Corps, most charismatic general of the Second World War, was glad to be summoned to the Fuehrer's headquarters in December 1943. The previous twelve months had not been happy ones.

Since his return from Africa in the spring of the year, he had spent some time in hospital, recovering from exhaustion following his efforts in the desert; had kicked

Sighted to fire along the beach, a German emplacement today.

his heels for a while at Hitler's Headquarters; and was, in November 1943, commanding an Army Group centred in Bavaria and Northern Italy.

This was not an active fighting command, and his term in office there was plagued with trouble from the S.S., the political soldiers formed from the ranks of the Nazi party.

There had been no S.S. formations in the Afrika Corps, a fact which had no doubt contributed to the relatively clean nature of the desert fighting. There had been no massacres of prisoners or reprisals against civilians under Rommel's command.

S.S. Divisions, while under Wehrmacht control for operations, were not under control in matters of discipline and this, plus their known brutality to prisoners and the local population, proved a continuous source of trouble for Rommel, particularly when he found his complaints about their behaviour were referred to political leaders such as Himmler, and there ignored. S.S. units, however unpopular, were nevertheless usually excellent fighting units, and through their political influence usually had the pick of manpower and equipment.

For many reasons Rommel was glad to leave Italy, and looked forward to the new appointment, outlined to him by the Fuehrer.

His initial task was to inspect the defences along the Atlantic Wall from Denmark to the Spanish Frontier, and report on their ability to repel the coming invasion.

Rommel was no stranger to the Atlantic Coast. In 1940, commanding the 7th Panzer Division, he had helped snuff out the last British resistance in France, when his division surrounded and attacked the 51st Highland Division, then making an epic stand at St. Valery.

Rommel himself led the German infantry in the final assault on the Highlanders' positions, and subsequently took 7th Panzer along the Normandy coast and up the Cotentin Peninsula to capture Cherbourg.

In 1944 Rommel began his task with a series of whirlwind inspection tours along the entire length of the Atlantic Wall. He was horrified by what he found, for in all but a few areas the Wall simply did not exist.

The major ports and certain possible Allied objectives such as the Channel ports and positions in the Pas de Calais, were well protected with heavy guns, emplacements and adequate garrisons secure in intricate defence systems, but elsewhere there were huge stretches of coast where the defences were no more than a few mines and some barbed wire, quite inadequate to deter an invader, let alone one that had the strength of the force now mustering in England.

Although by 1943 the shortage of war material for the German forces was becoming acute, the main blame for the lack of defences along the coast lay with the Oberkommando Wehrmacht (OKW) the German High Command, who since 1942 had made the fundamental mistake of believing their own propaganda.

Following the bloody repulse of the Dieppe Raid, Geobbels, Hitler's Minister of Propaganda had made great play with the proved invincibility of the Atlantic Wall, citing Dieppe as evidence of what would happen to any invader who dared put a foot on Fortress Europe. The Germans were bombarded with propaganda which seemed to bear out Hitler's claims that the Allies would never set foot in Europe until Hitler's V-weapons, long promised, were able to end the war.

Capped with a mine, this obstacle could sink any landing craft.

France had therefore been listed low in the priority scale and become a rest area for Divisions mauled on the Russian Front. The permanent garrison consisted largely of low grade divisions manned by Poles, Rumanians, elderly and unfit Germans and renegade Russians. Some indication of the diversity in these divisions is indicated by the fact that in some of their battalions, eight different types of paybook were necessary, for Russians, Cossacks, Armenians, Georgians, Turkmen, Tartars and so on. Such diversity was no source of strength.

The development of defences, especially beach obstacles and strong points, was hampered by a shortage of steel, concrete and manpower, for the main German labour force, the Todt Organisation, was busy repairing bomb damage in the Ruhr.

Rommel reported his findings to OKW and to Field Marshal Von Rundstedt, commanding Army Group West, but little was done to rectify matters.

He therefore decided to take a direct line in the affair and applied for and was given command of Army Group B consisting of three German Armies stationed between the Netherlands and the Loire. In this section the invasion would certainly come and Rommel would be the Commander of the anti-invasion forces. As Commander of Army Group B, Rommel was responsible directly to Von Rundstedt. There might have been friction between the two men, since Rommel had, in effect, gone over Von Rundstedt's head to obtain his command, and while Von Rundstedt was the doyen of the Officer Korps, Rommel was regarded in some Wehrmacht circles as an upstart, who had gained his rapid promotion by the favour of Hitler.

Von Rundstedt had, by this time, little interest left in fighting the war. His authority was continually undermined by interference from Hitler and he was quite content to let Rommel have a free hand if he wanted one. The disputes Rommel had with Von Rundstedt's headquarters, Army Group West, were over supplies and tactics, and his main opponent was the Commander of Panzer Forces in the West, Geyr Von Schweppenburg. They also disagreed on where the invasion would come.

Rommel's appreciation of the Allied intention fell somewhere between that of Hitler and the OKW. He felt that Normandy was more likely than the Pas de Calais, but decided that an assault around the mouth of the Somme was the most probable of all. It was in this area, and Normandy, that he concentrated his efforts, setting out to develop the defences without delay, using energy, ingenuity and his genius for improvisation, to overcome a chronic shortage of material.

Rommel's intention was to halt the invasion on the waterline, and here again his views were different from those of Von Rundstedt, most of the General Staff, and Geyr Von Schweppenburg.

Von Rundstedt felt that with over 1500 miles of coast to defend, and the Allied command of the sea, the invasion simply could not be prevented. He therefore did not propose to try and prevent the Allies getting ashore, but concentrated on defending major ports and building up, where permitted, a strategic reserve, which would, once the main part of the invasion had been located, move against it, and push the landing forces back into the sea.

This was a classic defensive strategy, and Rommel appreciated it, while totally disagreeing with the concept. He felt that the Allied Command of the air would be decisive and prevent the movement of a strategic reserve and that such forces as were able to move would be shattered by Allied air strikes before they got near the landing areas.

He intended to work well forward and defeat the invasion on the beaches, and in the first day. Within his own Command he made preparation to do just that, but his overall preparations were hampered by disagreements on the basic policy, particularly with the Geyr Von Schweppenburg, who controlled the best equipped divisions in the West, the Panzer divisions of the Waffen S.S.

Rommel and his superiors were still arguing the fundamental points of his policy when the Allied troops came ashore.

Apart from manpower, the Germans needed to develop their defences to a depth capable of bringing the invasion to a grinding halt.

Rommel's defences began below high water mark, in the area between the tides. Beams and tree trunks were driven deep into the sand, the tops projecting seawards and crowned with sharp steel cutters to rip open landing craft. Other poles were draped with fused mines. Concrete tank obstacles, obsolete ashore, were dragged into the sea to hamper ng craft beaching while navel mines were secured in the shallow coastal waters with lines attached to their horns. Most difficult of all to overcome was 'Element C'. This obstacle came in various forms and consisted of a heavy steel fence supported by wooden posts and mined. There were also steel girders welded together like enormous starfish, and wooden ramps, mines, barbed wire, Belgian gates, concrete dragon's teeth and fused shells.

These obstacles offered a number of possible terrors. They might succeed in sinking landing craft outright, or in blowing the occupants sky-high. They might impale the craft and expose them, stuck fast, to shell fire from the shore. They might force them to disembark the troops far out, beyond the obstacles at low tide, where they could be machine-gunned as they waded ashore. They might let craft in, but probably, in the confusion, the craft would not get out again to bring up reinforcements. At the very least, these underwater obstacles would considerably disrupt the landings. The beaches themselves were sewn with an assortment of anti-tank and personnel mines screened with wire and covered by guns, anti-tank emplacements, flame throwers and machine gun posts in reinforced concrete bunkers.

Rommel made great use of mines. In the four months before June, four million were laid along the Channel coast, and had time permitted he intended to lay between fifty and a hundred million mines before his preparations were complete. With mines, as with everything else, there was a shortage, which Rommel overcame by employing old French shells fused to explode on contact.

Minefields can be readily cleared unless they are covered by machine guns, so behind and above the beaches, Rommel constructed pill boxes and concrete emplacements for Spandau machine guns and artillery, notably the formidable 88mm anti-tank gun. These guns, and all the emplacements close to the shore, were sited to fire along the beach, the seaward wall protected by reinforced concrete many feet thick, covered and camouflaged with earth and sandbags, positioned to enfilade troops and tanks crossing the beach and to deny the invaders any exit from the

The drop zone of the 508 U.S. Parachute Infantry was flooded on D-Day.

landing beach, which was thereby converted into a killing-ground.

Beyond the beaches were more minefields and wire, and the trench lines of the defending infantry. Rommel instructed the coastal divisions to entrench everybody, including cooks, clerks and drivers, in deep dugouts with connecting passages, permitting movement from one post to another, with cover from enemy fire.

Inland, all open fields, likely spots for airborne landings, either by parachute or glider, were studded thickly with posts, designed to smash the gliders as they came down. These became known as Rommel's asparagus. The posts were strung with barbed wire and some were mined.

Along the Normandy coasts it was also possible to flood a number of areas, notably around Ste-Mere-Eglise and Carentan, where the American Paratroops would land, and in the east around Ranville, where the British 6th Airborne Division had tasks to perform.

These areas were flooded, either by

damming the rivers until the banks overflowed into the surrounding country, or by breaking the banks themselves allowing the water to flow out into the fields to a depth of between 2 and 4 feet.

The floodwater quickly became covered with weed, and was therefore almost invisible to Allied reconnaissance aircraft, which were now, as Spring began to break across the land, making regular flights over the invasion area.

They noted, among other things, the construction of battery positions, containing heavy guns, especially at Merville, east of Ouistreham, on the cliffs by Pointe du Hoc on the coast by the mouth of the Vire, and on the cliffs near Port en Bessin. These were thought to contain massive 155mm guns, with a range of 20 miles, enough to embarrass any invasion fleet anchored off the coast.

All these preparations and positions demanded men, especially trained fighting infantry and artillery men, who could hold their positions in spite of what came at them.

The Normandy coast was defended by the German 7th Army, which in the early Spring had five Infantry Divisions and one Panzer Division, the 21st, on or near the landing area. As the invasion drew near, Rommel reinforced these divisions and demanded that more forces should be made available. On D-Day the Germans had six Infantry Divisions, 21st Panzer, an Airborne Regiment and some Russian units actually in the invasion area, with three Infantry Divisions, a Parachute Division and two Panzer Units, the Panzer Lehr, and 12th S.S. Panzer in close support. Rommel would have preferred these last on the beaches, but permission to employ them was still waiting when the invasion came.

North of the 7th Army, lay the 15th Army, which had 250,000 men and two well equipped Panzer Divisions. However, 15th Army defended the Pas de Calais and Allied deception plans, plus a belief in the German High Command that this would be the invasion area, kept 15th Army out of the D-Day area until it was too late.

Throughout the Spring, Rommel and his men worked and waited. The defences grew and became more secure. The morale of the men improved as Rommel's efforts produced new equipment and their defences developed. As the Allies were lucky to have Eisenhower, so were the defenders of the Atlantic Wall lucky to have Rommel.

He was not an easy man to work with but he knew his job, and you knew where you were with him and what he wanted. In case there was any doubt, Rommel spelt out his attitude in detail.

'I give orders only when necessary. I expect them to be obeyed at once, and to the letter. No order shall be ignored, changed or delayed by lack of zeal or red tape.'

Rommel's intention was to defeat the Allies on the beaches and his men were to stay in position and carry out his intentions.

Although the defences were nowhere near complete when the attack came, they were vastly improved, manned by resolute troops, and to overcome them would be a mighty task indeed.

THE PLAN OF ATTACK

Now thrive the armourers . . .
for now sits expectation in the air.

The basis for OVERLORD was the COSSAC plan. COSSAC, apart from deciding the area of the assault, had analysed most of the problems the invaders would have to face and gone some way towards providing the answers. The main disagreement Eisenhower and Montgomery had with the COSSAC plan was with the proposed weight of the assault, calculated by COSSAC at three seaborne divisions and two airborne brigades, and with the size of the assault area, thirty miles of coast between the Orne and the Vire.

They felt that the weight was insufficient to resist the inevitable counter attacks and the area too small to deploy their forces and avoid confusion.

COSSAC were fully aware of the limitation of their plan, but the size of the assault was, at the time, necessarily restricted by a lack of suitable shipping. Shipping, transportation and supply played such a major part in OVERLORD that it received a separate code name, OPERATION NEPTUNE, and is fully discussed in the next chapter.

On taking up his appointment, Eisenhower had gone directly to Washington to confer with Roosevelt and Marshall, but he sent Montgomery ahead to London, instructing him to examine the COSSAC plan in detail, and make proposals for the necessary changes. Montgomery did so, deciding that whatever the difficulties, if OVERLORD were to succeed, then the whole invasion must be enlarged both in strength and area.

The point at issue went far beyond the problems of getting men to the coasts of France and putting them ashore.

It was necessary to examine the strategic objective of OVERLORD, the capture of Germany, and the ending of the Nazi regime, and then work back to the force necessary to achieve that end. A tactical defeat on the beaches would stop OVERLORD in its tracks, and even if, in the COSSAC manner, the force got ashore, Montgomery considered that to achieve the strategic objectives of the plan, the landings must be on a much larger scale. He therefore proposed to enlarge the assault force to five seaborne divisions, backed with three airborne divisions, two commando brigades, and detachments of their American equivalent, the United States Rangers.

Fortresses of the 8th U.S. Airforce
on their way to bomb targets in France.

Eisenhower and Montgomery watch a training exercise in England in 1944.

To broaden the area of attack and as a step towards the capture of Cherbourg, he suggested a coastal landing in the Cotentin, which would broaden the invasion front to about 50 miles. There would, of course, be gaps in this front, as dictated by the terrain, but the overall breadth could quickly be linked up by flank marches.

Eisenhower and the Combined Chiefs of Staff accepted these amendments, and Montgomery then proceeded to prepare plans for the actual landings, acting in fact, if not in name, as Commander in Chief, Ground Forces, for the invasion phase of OVER-LORD.

As Commander, 21st Army Group, he would anyway be in overall command of all armies, during the invasion phase, and as his ability to organise a set piece attack was unequalled in the Allied camp his instructions and advice to General Bradley, commanding the American 1st Army, were willingly accepted and adopted.

In outline, Montgomery's plan called for

Spitfire strike against installations in France.

the airborne divisions to drop on the night of D-1, sealing the flanks and vital features of the invasion area before the seaborne forces came ashore the following morning. These were to establish two bridgeheads, one in the Cotentin peninsula around Ste-Mere-Eglise, as a step towards cutting the Peninsula and seizing Cherbourg, the other on the north coast, between the Orne and Vire, aiming to capture Caen, Bayeux and Isigny, and gain sufficient ground inland to let the follow-up divisions get ashore without confusion.

As Spring arrived in 1944, work on achieving these objectives began.

One of the earliest lessons learned about a cross-channel invasion, was the importance of air superiority. This the Allies had, provided the weather was good enough to allow their aircraft to operate. Given that the Germans were operating on interior lines and could build up their forces more quickly than the Allies unless prevented by Airforce interdiction, it was generally agreed that air power would be the decisive element in the early

Heavy air attacks destroyed French rolling stock.

days of the invasion, until the Allies could land sufficient forces to outnumber their opponents.

Eisenhower had two air fleets under his direct control, the American 9th, and the British 2nd Tactical. These were largely equipped with medium bombers, fighters and fighter bombers, and designed to provide air cover and tactical air support to Naval and ground forces.

Eisenhower also demanded and obtained, for the invasion period, operational control of the two strategic bomber forces operating out of Britain at the time, the American 8th Airforce and R.A.F. Bomber Command. These were equipped with long range bombers and were busy at the time destroying German industry in the Ruhr and elsewhere, as part of the long term plan for paralysing German industry and thus ending the war.

Under Eisenhower's direction they switched their attacks in the Spring of 1944 to the marshalling yards and the rail links between France and the German homeland,

In D-Day markings, a Typhoon goes in to attack.

with a view to reducing the build up of German forces and material in France prior to D-Day and their subsequent reinforcement after it.

In this task the air forces were highly successful. By mid-May rail traffic between France and Germany had fallen by fifty per cent, while inside France it was down to twenty per cent of the January level. The tactical fighter and fighter bomber forces joined in strafing train and troop convoys, and shooting up stations and rail junctions.

Over 1500 French locomotives were destroyed, representing sixty per cent of those available, and other rolling stock suffered in proportion.

Another Airforce task was to assist in the sealing off of Normandy beaches to the invasion by destroying the bridges across the Seine on the open flank of the invasion forces. Bridges are difficult to bomb accurately and all were heavily defended, but here again the aircraft pressed home their attacks until by June 1st only three of the

Loading rockets into a Typhoon.

twenty-six bridges over the Seine were usable, and those were damaged and still under attack. This action was a vital part in the pre-invasion preparation, for the Germans would need their bridges to pump forces into Normandy, or for a speedy withdrawal if their position there became untenable.

The Air Force efforts in France were supplemented by the operations of the French Resistance, the Maquis. Reinforced by special parachuted teams of British and American soldiers, they began, as the invasion date drew near, a series of attacks on the communications networks in France, destroying in particular stocks of spares, cranes, and maintenance facilities, until bomb damage that would have taken two days to repair in January, was taking two weeks by June.

Thanks to all this, the Wehrmacht's ability to react against the invaders was already severely crippled before the first invader set foot in France.

The detailed tasks of the various assault

divisions will be described in later chapters, for the main pre-occupation of the planning staff of SHAEF during the Winter and early Spring of 1944 was to increase the weight of the assault and see the men safely ashore. The NEPTUNE staff were in difficulties finding the shipping for the extra divisions and at the end of January it was decided that the invasion must be put back one month to a date on or about the 1st June.

This would, apart from giving the Anglo-American forces more time, enable the invasion to coincide with the Russian Summer offensive. This gave everyone a little more breathing space, and training now commenced on detailed aspects of the plan.

The lessons learned on the Dieppe Raid were proving really vital now, in particular the necessity of giving the infantry armoured support in the moment of assault, and of the need for some sort of armoured vehicles specialised to get the tanks and other vehicles off the beaches, and deployed in support of the infantry.

Montgomery's plan here was highly original, for he stood the normal concept on its head and decided to land his tanks first, followed by the specialised armour, variously designed to deal with different types of beach opposition and obstacles, then regular infantry to mop up, and finally Commandos to deal with the strong points, and the necessary flank deployment. This is almost exactly the opposite of the accepted order, and shows a high degree of original thinking, with an ability to face facts however unpalatable, and find solutions, however radical.

Montgomery realised that tanks would have to clear a way through the beach defences for the infantry who would otherwise be cut down, as at Dieppe, by machine gun fire from concrete emplacements, but also that the tanks themselves would be neutralised by the defences unless some means could be found of quickly overcoming the obstacles that Rommel would have prepared to stop them on the beaches.

He had his answer in a wide range of specialised armoured vehicles in a unique formation, the 79th Armoured Division, commanded by Major-General Sir Percy Hobart, a pioneer of armoured warfare. In the thirties, Hobart's ideas for the use of armour had been so revolutionary that the War Office rewarded him with an early retirement, and in 1942 he was serving his country in the only post then open to him, as a corporal in the Home Guard.

He was rescued from this oblivion by Winston Churchill who directed him to use his ingenuity in the development of armoured devices for use in the forthcoming invasion. Hobart's machines, known generally as 'The Funnies' were to play a vital part on the fire swept beaches of Normandy.

The main item in his armoury, was the Duplex-Drive or D-D, swimming tank. Developed from river crossing techniques, the D-D tank was usually a Sherman, the main Allied battle tank. This floated inside a large canvas apron hung round the chassis, which held the tank suspended inside the canvas screen with the turret below the waterline. It looked hazardous, and indeed, if the screen was damaged in any way, the tank would quickly sink, usually drowning the crews. The canvas screen was therefore vital, for thus supported, and driven by propellers, the tank could swim ashore, drop the canvas screen and go straight into action.

The big advantage of the D-D, apart from

D-D tanks, with screens up.

A facine tank.

Filling in the crater.

51

surprise, was that it enabled tanks to support infantry in the assault in places where it was impossible for large tank carrying vessels to beach. The D-D could be launched in deep water and go ashore with the infantry landing craft. Virtually invisible it was calculated to give the defender a nasty turn when it lumbered out of the waves and opened fire. The Germans suspected the existence of such a vehicle but until they appeared on D-Day, had no definite proof.

About nine hundred D-D tanks, mostly converted Shermans, were used on D-Day, by the British and American Armies.

In addition the 79th contained a wide variety of obstacle clearing tanks.

They had tanks, bearing a massive flail, that could beat a path through minefields. There were 'Bobbins', which could lay a path across mud or quicksand, and 'Petards' that could blast a hole in pillboxes or blast a path through concrete sea walls. They had fearful flame throwing tanks to scorch out machine gun nests, bridge carrying tanks to mount walls or cross gaps, and 'Fascines' to fill in a shell or bomb crater, and many more. The British organised these devices into their assault plans loading them into the ships in the order they would be needed ashore.

The first obstacle might be a patch of tank bogging mud, so the first out would be a 'Bobbin', to lay a path across it. Then followed a flail to beat a path through a minefield up to the sea wall, clearing a path for a bridge building tank which then helped to scale it. Up would go a 'Petard' or flame tank to deal with the pillbox on top, while a 'Fascine' would lay its logs down to reduce the drop on the far side. Behind them would come the other armour, streaming through the breach thus made in the Atlantic

The bridgelaying tank: *Constructed on a Churchill chassis, this tank could bridge gaps of up to 25 feet. These tanks could also carry facines to fill in craters.*

The Churchill AVRE (Armoured vehicle Royal Engineers) Petard Tank: *Mounting a 25 pd. spigot mortar, this tank could blast a hole in sea walls, and knock out pillboxes and blockhouses.*

Churchill MK VIII Crocodile: *The flame throwing tank, that could pump 400 gallons of flame, up to 120 yards, and was used with devastating effect against pillboxes and machine gun posts.*

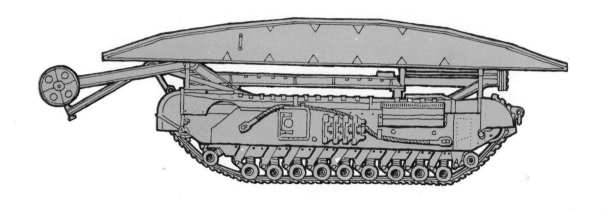

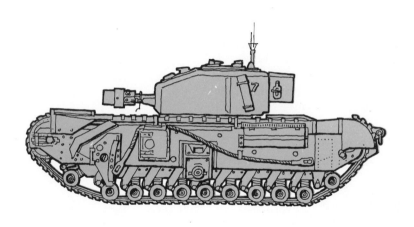

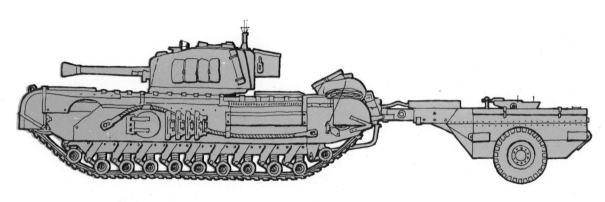

Wall with the minimum of loss or delay.

The 'Funnies' were demonstrated and offered to the American assault forces under Bradley, but he turned them down, partly because they were in the main mounted on British Churchill tanks, which would cause spare and maintenance problems, partly because his beaches were more open and not backed with the small towns that lay along the British front, but mostly because he considered them an unnecessary frill. He favoured a frontal assault by infantry in the good old manner, and relied on the guts and fighting ability of his infantry to get them ashore. He took the D-D tanks, and declined the rest. One thing Bradley did want and the British could not supply were 'Firefly' tanks, which were converted Shermans mounting a 17 pounder anti-tank gun. Only 'Fireflies' could match the powerful German 'Tiger' and 'Panther' tanks, and there were not enough of them to go round.

One of the U.S. 1st Army's tasks lay in the Cotentin, where they had to land, turn North, and take Cherbourg, the main port in the invasion coast. Dieppe had shown that to seize a major port in working order was highly unlikely, and the Allied answer to this was to take floating ports with them in the form of Mulberry Harbours which, as basically a Naval venture, will be described in the next chapter.

Nevertheless, Cherbourg as the biggest port in the area was a vital objective, and it might be less strongly defended on the landward side, quickly taken and cleared for Allied use.

Montgomery proposed that the two American Airborne Divisions, the 101st and 82nd, should land, the first around Carentan to seal off the base of the Cotentin, the 82nd to land astride the River Merderet and take

The D.D. Tank: *Shown here with the skirt erected, the D.D. or Duplex Drive swimming tank, was the big surprise weapon on D-Day. Over 900 were used on the British and American beaches.*

The Bobbin: *Soft sand, mud or shale could bog a tank down, so this version unrolled a convas mat in front, and thus passed over onto firmer ground.*

Sherman MK II Crab: *The Crab or flail tank, could beat a path through minefields, the heavy chains detonating the mines in its path, and clearing a way for other tanks or infantry.*

54

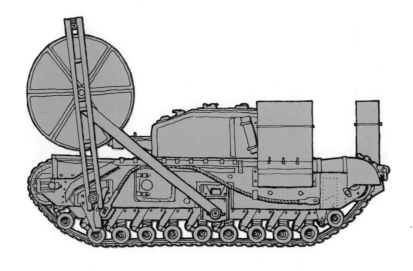

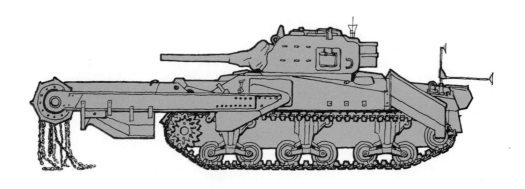

A bobbin tank in action.

Ste-Mere-Eglise, thus cutting communications with Cherbourg. They would also eliminate coastal batteries, and seize the exits to the beaches on the east coast of the peninsula where at H-Hour on D-Day, the American 4th Division would come ashore. Thus, with luck, the Cherbourg Peninsula could be quickly cleared of enemy, and the port fall into Allied hands.

This proposal for the use of the airborne division met with strenuous opposition from the Allied Air Commander, Air Chief Marshal Leigh Mallory, whose aircraft would drop the paratroops and tow the gliders that carried their airlanding brigades and heavy equipment. He felt that the anti-aircraft defences in the Cherbourg area and the unsuitability of the terrain for airborne landings could cause casualties of up to seventy-five per cent of the landing force.

There were suitable drop zones in the flat country around Carentan but these had been flooded by the Germans.

These floods formed a vital part in

The Caen Canal Bridge.

Montgomery's plan. Had the Allies landed outside the peninsula, the floods at the base would be a useful defence for the Germans. He proposed, by landing in the peninsula, to turn them into an obstacle to German re-inforcement by taking Carentan and defending the north line of the flood waters, while other forces took Cherbourg. Leigh Mallory's objectives were over-ruled and were in the event unfounded.

The outline of the invasion tasks now began to emerge.

At midnight on D-1, the three airborne divisions would land by parachute or glider, the British 6th Airborne astride the Orne, the American 82nd and 101st at the base of the Cotentin in the West.

At 0630 hrs. the seaborne landings would commence on a series of beach areas, starting in the West where the U.S. 4th Infantry Division would land on the east coast of the Cotentin. At the same time 20 miles away on the Calvados coast, the American 1st and 29th Infantry Divisions would go ashore.

These landings were code named UTAH and OMAHA.

4th Infantry were to link up with 82nd Airborne around Ste-Mere-Eglise, and seize a bridgehead in the peninsula.

At OMAHA 1st Infantry were to swing east to link up with the British at Port en Bassin, while the 29th Division, landing later, were to swing west and take Isigny aiming at a link up with the 101st Airborne in Carentan.

Between UTAH and OMAHA, on the promontory of Pointe du Hoc, it was thought that a battery of heavy guns commanded the ship assembly areas for both beaches. This battery was to be heavily bombed then assaulted by three companies of the 2nd U.S. Rangers. The fishing port of Port en Bessin was the dividing line between the Anglo-American Armies and was to be captured by No.47 (Royal Marine) Commando. 47 Commando would land on the west flank of the British 2nd Army and make a 10 mile advance through enemy territory to attack Port en Bessin from the rear.

The British Second Army, commanded by General Sir Miles Dempsy, would land two Corps, on three beaches on a thirty mile front between Arromanches and Ouistreham.

On the western beach, code-named GOLD, the 50th (Northumbrian) Division of XXX Corps would land between Le Hamel and La Riviere, drive west to meet the Americans, and inland to take Bayeux.

Next, on JUNO, the Canadian 3rd Division, later to form part of the Canadian Army, would land between Graye sur Mere and St. Aubin, and proceed inland towards Caen.

Also at St. Aubin, No.48 (Royal Marine) Commando would come ashore, behind the Canadians, to turn left and clear defences along the coast and link up with No.41

(Royal Marine) Commando which had landed on the west flank of the British 3rd Division at Lion sur Mer. 3rd Division's beach ran from Lion to the outskirts of Ouistreham, and was code-named SWORD.

The town of Ouistreham would be captured by No.4 (Army) Commando of 1st S.S. (Commando) Brigade. The remainder of 1st Commando Brigade would land later, and advance to link up with 6th Airborne in their positions astride the Orne, and the canal that linked Ouistreham and Caen.

Thus the D-Day bridgeheads would run from the high ground around Ranville east of the Orne to the floodwaters of the Vire around Isigny, north across them to Carentan, and the American drop zones and finally to the 4th Division at Ste-Mere-Eglise. All being well this line should be complete on D + 1. A study of the endpaper maps, at this point, will clarify the Allied objectives for the reader.

There were, in this, as in all plans, a large number of imponderables. First, there was the weather. An analysis of meteorological records seemed to suggest that the May-June period, after the early Spring gales, offered the best chance of fulfilling the necessary requirements for a successful landing. These were for at least four calm days, with the sea no rougher than a slight chop, good visibility of not less than 3 miles, a cloud base of more than 3000 feet and, for the paratroops, a surface wind of not more than 15 miles per hour. While the May-June period offered a chance of this, the odds were still calculated at 12-1 against.

A further requirement for the paratroops was a late rising moon, so that the parachute aircraft had cover of darkness for the flight, and moonlight during the drop, and finally the optimum conditions for the seaward assault called for half tide conditions around dawn.

There were a number of opinions about the most suitable landing time, and half tide on the flood, only offered the least problems for the best advantage. At low tide, while most beach and underwater obstacles would be visible, the troops would have to advance 500 yards, over a quarter of a mile across flat beach under fire before they got to cover in the dunes. At full tide, the obstacles would be covered, difficult to locate and might be expected to cause havoc among the assault craft. Beside this, the narrow strips of beach above the high water mark, would be insufficient to let the troops, tanks and vehicles deploy.

Therefore half tide, and in June the first days when the moon would be suitable and it would be half tide around dawn, would be on the morning of the 4th, 5th and 6th of June. Because of the extent of the NEPTUNE area, it also followed that to land at half tide the British forces in the east would have to land one hour later than the Americans in the west, as the incoming tide flooded up the Channel.

The second great imponderable was the reaction of the enemy.

Allied Intelligence was reasonably well informed about German troops' movements, strengths and dispositions, but the information on which their estimates were based was difficult to collect, and delayed in transmission. Their Intelligence could not be right up to date, and everyone was painfully aware that the unexpected appearance of even one Panzer Division in the wrong place could have a serious effect on the landing.

All that the Allied Commanders could do was to realise that, as their air reconnaissance revealed, the Atlantic Wall was getting stronger every day, anticipate that enemy manpower would grow as the invasion they were expecting drew near, and take every step possible to disperse the enemy forces and take him by surprise. Knowing that the two best invasion areas, Normandy or the Pas de Calais would be as obvious to German planners as they were to the Allies, great pains were taken to hint discreetly, and apparently accidentally, at a mere diversion in Normandy, followed by the major assault in the Pas de Calais. This deception plan was known as 'OPERATION FORTITUDE'.

Somewhat obvious preparations were established in South East England. Dummy landing craft were moved in the Thames and Medway, and dummy gliders appeared on the airfields of Essex and Kent. An elaborate signalling unit in Kent, transmitted Montgomery's coded signals, creating a large volume of radio traffic for the Germans to monitor, but the signals were sent by telephone from Montgomery's actual headquarters near Southampton. General Patton's 3rd Army, one of the follow up forces, did assemble in Kent, and their tanks and field parks were seen by German reconnaissance aircraft making quick darts across the Channel. These aircraft were not chased with any vigour. Meanwhile, in neutral capitals all over the world, German agents were receiving hints that the Pas de Calais would be the big attack area and any information to the contrary was part of a cunning Allied plot. Even the air attacks were made to contribute to this deception so that for every ton of bombs dropped on Normandy, four tons went down in the Pas de Calais, where there were in any case, many more targets.

In spite of Rommel's utmost efforts the

defences of Normandy were less than twenty per cent complete when the invasion came, but the deception plans played a major part, not only in dispersing his strength before the invasion, but in forcing him to keep divisions in the North after the landings in anticipation of the expected major assault, when they could have been fighting the real invasion in Normandy.

Along with deception went security. In February 1944, the British Isles were sealed, and no civilian traffic was allowed between the U.K. and neutral countries like Eire, or Portugal, which swarmed with German agents. In April the British coast was closed up to ten miles inland from the Wash to Lands End. British civilians were subjected to further restrictions in the use of the post and telephones, to free the communications networks for military use, while all overseas mail, even diplomatic bags, was either stopped completely or subjected to censorship.

Meanwhile, throughout the Spring, the Allied armies were training, rehearsing their assault plans, and preparing their vehicles and weapons. Throughout May, at ports all over the country, the ships and landing craft were being loaded with vehicles and heavy equipment.

On 1st June the troops went into special camps near their embarkation points. There they received their final briefing, drew French money and were subject to complete security control. No messages, letters or 'phone calls could be made, and they were only allowed out for route marches. They were able to inspect models of the Atlantic Wall and see how and where they were to attack it, and the part that every tank and man would play in doing so. Montgomery visited many of the assault units, right down to battalion level, often called the men round his jeep to give them some orders for the manner of their attack. Montgomery knew that all plans are fallible in some degree, that in the end most battles are soldiers' battles, fought out, as the situation dictates, by the men on the spot.

As the infantry went on board their ships, and the Naval bombardment forces sailed south from their bases at Scapa, Belfast and the Clyde, everything now depended on the weather.

D-Day was scheduled for Monday, 5th June, when moon and tides would be favourable. The final command to 'carry out OPERATION OVERLORD', must come from SHAEF not less than thirty-six hours before H-Hour. Throughout most of May the weather had been perfect, but at the start of June it began to get unsettled, until on Saturday, 3rd June, with only forty-eight hours to go, the weather broke.

A convoy at sea.

OPERATION NEPTUNE

'Do but think,
You stand upon the rivage and behold,
A city, on the inconstant bellows dancing
For so appears this fleet majestical.'

The Royal Navy has been landing troops in France for centuries and had, long ago, worked out a basic routine for such amphibious operations, and in particular, had established the point at which their responsibility in an assault ended, and that of the Army began. This was at the High Water Mark of Ordinary Spring Tides or HWMOST. The Naval part of OVERLORD, OPERATION NEPTUNE, therefore, was to convey the Allied Liberation Army from ports in Britain, up to HWMOST on the Normandy beaches, to support them on the way in, and supply them thereafter.

To do this would require an immense fleet of ships and landing craft, and, of necessity, most of these would have to be British. To explain this, we must hark back to the American Admiral King, for the shortage of landing craft which had frustrated COSSAC's planners, and was to perplex OVERLORD's, was one of allocation, not of availability. Most of the larger landing craft then in service were American built. The British shipyards were at the time fully engaged in repairing war damaged vessels, building convoy escorts, and more particularly, in fabricating the parts for the Mulberry Harbours. There was little capacity for the construction of a fleet of landing craft, although many craft were constructed by factories, as far inland as Reading.

There was, however, flowing from the American shipyards a sufficiency of landing craft to meet all the Allied requirements, but as the allocation of craft to theatre depended on Admiral King, the European theatre tended to get very little, notably of the all important tank landing ships (L.S.T's). There is no need to labour this point, the figures speak for themselves.

On 1st May, 1944 the U.S. Navy had 10,000 landing craft of various types in service, and of these only 1,400 were allocated to OVERLORD, the major Allied amphibious operation of the war and OPERATION ANVIL, the invasion of the South of France, a concurrent and supporting operation. It was this shortage finally forced the OVERLORD planners to make adjustments to their plan.

D-Day went back to June, which allowed an extra month to produce craft and train crews, while ANVIL, which was to have been launched at the same time as OVERLORD was delayed until enough craft could be spared from OVERLORD to take the armies ashore in the South of France.

The command structure for NEPTUNE was as follows:

S.H.A.E.F.

C-in-C Allied Naval Forces
Admiral Sir Bertram Ramsey R.N.

Western Task Force (US)
Rear Admiral A. G. Kirk (USN)

Eastern Task Force (RN)
Rear Admiral Sir Phillip Vian (RN)

The Western task force would take the Americans ashore on OMAHA and UTAH, and Admiral Vian's force would escort the British to GOLD, JUNO, and SWORD. Under command of the two task forces were separate bombardment fleets, allocated to the various beaches, and called Force O, U, G, S, and J after their respective landing areas. Each beach area had a Headquarters control vessel, and a variety of support craft, firing rockets, or anti-aircraft guns.

Convoy escort.

These various Forces had under command for the assault, a total of 1,213 warships, from battleships to midget submarines and 4,126 landing ships and landing carft. There would, in addition, be another 1,000 vessels, involved in supply and in the Mulberry project, plus merchantmen, command and close support vessels, a total in all of over 6,000 ships and vessels of various types.

About seventy per cent of these were British or Canadian, the rest from either the U.S. Navy, the Free French, Norwegian or Dutch Navies. This was the largest fleet that ever put to sea, a vast armada that filled every port, roadstead and bay in the South of England, in the weeks before D-Day.

The invasion plan issued by Admiral Ramsey for the guidance of his captains ran, with all its various appendices, to 700 foolscap pages, a sight which so jolted his sailors that a directive had to be issued advising them that they need only read, learn, and inwardly digest, those parts directly concerned with their own activities. Even so,

it proved a lot to learn, and still provides a fair indicator of the inevitable complexity of OPERATION NEPTUNE.

The Naval Forces may, for clarity, be divided into two parts, warships and launching craft. The warships, which had the task of bombarding the beaches, and counter battery fire against shore artillery, included seven battleships, two monitors, twenty-three cruisers, one hundred and five destroyers, one hundred and eighty-nine minesweepers, and so on down to two midget submarines of the Royal Navy X20 and X23. These ships had, firstly to sweep mines from the path of the invasion convoys, protect the landing craft, bombard shore batteries and targets before and during the infantry assault, and supply Naval gunfire support as the battle ashore developed. Naval gunfire support was, next to air-power, to prove decisive in breaking up German counter attacks on the beachhead.

The landing craft were of wide variety. Largest, and most important were the L.S.T's of which there were two hundred and

Rocket landing craft, with more fire power than a cruiser.

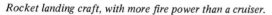

thirty-six in the assault, carrying the tanks and armour. They were supported by eight hundred and thirty-seven L.C.T's, the smaller Landing Craft, Tank. The infantry went ashore in a variety of craft, ranging from attack transports, landing craft, personnel, (L.C.P's), Landing Craft Assault (L.C.A's), Landing Ships Infantry (L.S.L) and Landing Craft Infantry (L.C.I's). There were also the support landing craft, Land Craft Rocket (L.C.R's), Landing Craft Guns (L.C.G's) and Landing Craft Flak (L.C.F's), these latter firing mainly anti-aircraft guns.

The L.C.I's which conveyed many of the infantry ashore had one great drawback, for instead of a ramp in the bows to let the troops out at about water level, they were equipped with two gangplanks, lowered from the bows, which reached from the deck to the sea. Down these gangplanks the heavily ladened infantry had to file, each carrying about 60 lbs of kit. Getting on to the gangplank was difficult, while getting down it without falling headlong into the sea, could

only be accomplished at a run. To run down a wet launching plank 18 inches wide with a load of kit and land chest deep in turbulent water, was a daunting way to go to war.

Had it not been for the decision to postpone the invasion for a month it is doubtful if Ramsey could have found enough shipping to convey the assault forces ashore for Eisenhower's requirements called for the Navies to land 175,000 men, 1,500 tanks, 3,000 guns and 10,000 assorted trucks, jeeps and unarmoured vehicles in the first 24 hours. To get some idea of this, it might help to realise that the American infantry alone for the UTAH and OMAHA assaults, would have filled 200 large troop trains. To make room for all the men and equipment it was necessary to cut the transport requirements of the assault divisions to the bone.

Onto the ships, apart from troops, weapons and transport went everything the armies might need, including a million gallons of drinking water. In adding to the landing operations the Navy were responsible for the

The Mulberry harbour.

design and construction of the Mulberry Harbours. The Mulberrys, artificial harbours that could be floated across the Channel and sunk in position on the other side, were originally proposed by Churchill, and later taken up by John Hughes Hallet, who had been Naval Force Commander at Dieppe. In 1942, after Dieppe, such ports became vital, and construction had been proceeding in prefabricated units all over the U.K. throughout 1943. The plan called for two Mulberrys to be positioned, one off OMAHA, for the Americans, and one off Arromanches for the British. Each would enclose an area about the

size of Dover Harbour, and accommodate ships of up to medium tonnage. The unloading piers were arranged so that they could float up and down with the tides, which in the Channel have a rise and fall of 19 feet. The outer breakwaters, or 'Gooseberries' were composed of sunken merchantmen, and these would in addition provide shelter for the landing craft in the event of sudden gales. Once constructed it was hoped that 7,000 tons of supplies could be unloaded daily through each port.

The Mulberrys' components came to 400 separate units, totalling one and a half million tons. It took 160 tugs and 10,000 men to get them in position, and regrettably, they lasted in full use for less than two weeks. On 19th June, a fierce three-day gale destroyed the American Mulberry off OMAHA and severely damaged the British one at Arromanches. The American one was abandoned, and although the one at Arromanches continued to function, it was discovered that cargo ships could be beached at UTAH and unloaded directly into trucks as the tide fell, to float off again, empty, on the next flood. Nevertheless, although of limited use, the Mulberrys were vital while they lasted and their existence gave confidence to the staff at SHAEF who, when planning the assault, knew they would have no port to supply the armies unless they took one with them.

Another unique invention was PLUTO, the Pipe Line Under the Ocean. A force that would contain 15,000 vehicles on D-Day alone and thousands more with every day that passed thereafter, would have a tremendous thirst for petrol, a thirst that could hardly be quenched by the use of tankers operating through Mulberrys or over open beaches. The planners answer to this was PLUTO.

As soon as Port en Bessin was captured by 47 (Royal Marine) Commando, a fuel depot was to be established. Here, where the U.S. and British sections met, it could hopefully supply both armies. And here an armoured pipeline, laid under the sea, could receive fuel pumped from the tankers lying offshore.

Later, at Querqueville near Cherbourg, the first cross Channel pipeline, laid from the Isle of Wight came ashore. Eventually there were four PLUTO pipelines, and their daily deliveries of 2,500 tons of petrol kept the armies moving until the ports were opened up.

The Navy had one other small but vital task during the landings. The two midget submarines X20 and X23, were to mark the beaches off JUNO and SWORD, surfacing as darkness fell and shining green lights seaward to bring the landing craft in at the right place. By mid-May the craft were beginning to load up at ports and improvised landing 'hards' all over England. At the end of May the troop carrying vessels assembled in their respective ports, ready to embark the Armies for the assault. Broadly speaking the American Forces were assembled in the west, in Dorset, Devon and Cornwall, while the British and Canadians embarked between Southampton and Newhaven. As the ships loaded, they moved out to anchor in the bays and roadsteads offshore, a vast armada crammed with men and equipment ready for the great assault. On 1st June Admiral Ramsey moved his operational headquarters to Portsmouth, and on the 2nd, the capital ships of the Fleet began to sail south from their bases in the North of Ireland, and Scotland.

At midnight on 2nd June X20 and X23 sailed for their stations off the coast of Normandy, and slowly, but with ever increasing momentum the invasion began to gather speed. On the 3rd the Infantry went aboard their ships, and even as the weather began to deteriorate and whitecapped waves rose in the Channel, the most Western invasion convoys set sail from Falmouth in Cornwall. D-Day was still planned for dawn on 5th June. Butting into a westerly gale they turned east, towards their assembly areas off Normandy.

Meanwhile, at Eisenhower's headquarters, the atmosphere was becoming fraught. All that could be done to make the invasion work had been done, but no one could arbitrate for the weather. All attention was fixed on Group Captain Stagg, R.A.F. head of the SHAEF Meteorological Unit. His forecast in the early hours of 4th June was one of continuing bad weather for the next three days, with low cloud, which would virtually ground the Air Forces. This last was the critical factor since only the Air Forces could prevent the massive German counter attacks that were sure to follow the landings.

Time was now getting very short, and at dawn on the 4th Eisenhower postponed the invasion by twenty-four hours, and recalled the vessels then at sea. One group of ships, Force U2, bound for UTAH, could not be contacted by radio, and had to be chased and turned back by destroyers. For the soldiers, crammed into the troop decks, apprehensive and seasick, the delay seemed unendurable.

Throughout Sunday 4th June, the storm grew worse with heavy seas pounding the beaches on both sides of the Channel. At 9.00 p.m. that evening, Eisenhower and his Generals met again, and Group Captain Stagg gave another forecast on the weather. He had one slight chance to offer; the possibility that after the present storm had passed, in about twenty-four hours, there would be a period of reasonable weather, with moderate cloud, until the evening of 6th June. It was a small chance and a great risk, but alternatives were equally unpalatable. The ships were ready to sail, and if this chance went by, there would be a delay of at least two weeks until the tides would again be favourable. The soldiers could not be kept aboard ship for that length of time, and security could not guarantee to keep the time and place of the invasion secret much longer. By dawn of 5th June, when SHAEF met again for the final discussions the issue could no longer be postponed. Small chance it may be but it was all Stagg could offer. 'O.K.' said Eisenhower, 'We'll go'.

D-Day would be Tuesday the Sixth of June.

Two hours later the convoys began to sail, preceeded by the minesweepers that sweep the channels clear for them. The mine-sweepers were off the Normandy coast by the early evening of 5th June, close enough to distinguish houses on shore. They seemed to be ignored by the Germans.

Just after midnight, the troopships began to arrive at their assembly points, quietly, and without lights. There was no confusion, and in spite of a heavy sea, the grouping of vessels at their assembly areas went according to plan.

There was no opposition from the German Navy. Their E-boats stayed snug in their harbours at Cherbourg and Le Havre convinced that no invasion fleet could have sailed in such weather. Even Field Marshal Rommel thought the invasion unlikely, so much so, that he went home to visit his wife in Germany on her birthday.

The only sound that disturbed the night was the steady drone of aircraft engines, as the bombers of the 9th Air Force and Bomber Command began the attacks on the German batteries and beach defences. These raids had been going on for months and caused no particular alarm.

Far away, on the east and western flanks of the invasion fleet, were more aircraft, many more, but these carried not bombs, but men. At midnight, by parachute or glider, 20,000 Allied soldiers of the three airborne divisions landed in Normandy. OPERATION OVER-LORD had begun.

THE AMERICAN AIRDROPS

'Now entertain conjecture of a time,
When creeping murmur, and the poring
dark,
Fill the wild vessel of the universe . . .
and so our scene must to the
battle fly.

The two American airborne divisions, the 82nd, commanded by Major General Matthew B. Ridgeway, and the 101st, commanded by Major General Maxwell Taylor were to land in the Cotentin in support of the American seaborne landings on UTAH. There had been considerable controversy over the decision to use them in the Cotentin, for the area was well defended with anti-aircraft guns, and the ground unsuitable for our landings. Those flat, open areas that were suitable had already been flooded by the Germans, or studded with mines and booby-trapped anti-invasion posts. Air Marshal Leigh Mallory who objected to the drop, was eventually over-ruled, although the plan was modified in part, to allow for at least some of the difficulties he anticipated.

For a successful drop, paratroopers ideally require a flat open plain without rivers, trees or man-made obstacles. For them to jump successfully the aircraft have to fly at not above 1,000 feet, upwind, across this plain at as slow a speed as possible, and not faster than 120 m.p.h., while the troopers jump as fast as possible, one after the other. The faster

they can get out of the aircraft, and the slower the aircraft is going at a low height, the closer they will be when they arrive on the ground, enabling them to assemble quickly in orderly groups and set about their tasks. A parachute drop is simply one way of getting an infantry battalion into action, and is not supposed to send individual soldiers all over the landscape.

The two American airborne divisions had had quite a different war up to this time. The 82nd had been in action before at Salerno and in Sicily where they had been severely scattered in the drop and had a very bad time. They were an experienced and fully trained formation, and had plenty of know-how to back their training. On the other hand, the 101st, or the 'Screaming Eagles' as they preferred to call themselves, were a new formation and would be going into action on D-Day for the first time. Each division consisted of three regiments, each of three battalions supported by airborne artillery, engineer and medical units, and as with the British Airborne forces, delivered men to the battlefield in gliders as well as by parachute.

An American paratrooper, fully equipped.

The 82nd's task on D-Day was to land around Ste-Mere-Eglise, to seize and hold the crossroads there, and like the British in the East, seize or destroy the bridges over the Merderet and Douve rivers, thus isolating the western flank of the invasion, and making a step towards cutting the peninsula.

The 101st were to land north and east of Carentan, capture that town, and seize the landward exits of the causeways across the marsh behind UTAH Beach.

Originally the 82nd had been going to land on the west coast of the Cotentin cutting the west coast road to Cherbourg at La Haye du Puits, but this plan had been abandoned after Leigh Mallory's objections. The cutting of the Cotentin Peninsula and the subsequent capture of Cherbourg would depend, not on the chance of a successful airborne coup de main on D-Day but on the speed with which the Americans could advance through the dense countryside of the Normandy bocage.

The Americans would take off from airfields in Southern England at midnight on 5th June and fly a circle route to their drop zones, approaching the Cotentin from the West flying north of the Channel Islands and across, rather than down, the Peninsula. This avoided flying over the formidable guns of Cherbourg, but meant that the aircraft would be over land for barely seven minutes, and over their drop zones for less than two. Anyone jumping late stood a fair chance of landing in the sea. They also flew with the prevailing wind, which in many cases meant the aircraft were flying at speeds in excess of 150 m.p.h., too fast for a good close drop. It will be seen, therefore, that the successful use of the airborne forces on the ground, depends very much on an accurate and controlled drop by the airforce, for if the troops were

scattered, they can never find each other in the dark, enemy-held countryside on which they descend.

The Allied planners were well aware of this, and held, prior to D-Day a series of night exercises, with mass parachute drops, to train the pilots in their duties, and to rehearse pathfinding and drop-zone indicating techniques. Unfortunately, it is never possible to reproduce the nervousness and excitement generated by the operational drop itself. All airborne divisions included pathfinder units, small bodies of highly trained men, who dropped ahead of the main body to locate the drop zone, and mark it accurately with lights and radio beacons, thereby bringing the main force in on their objectives. These exercises went reasonably well, and no real problems of pathfinding or drop zone marking were expected on D-Day.

The delay in launching the invasion came as no surprise to the Airborne Forces. They could see the wind bending the branches of the trees, and whipping out the windsocks on the airfields, along the runways of which their aircraft by hundreds stood in line, ready for the take off. A parachutist very quickly learns to study the weather, as his life and limbs depend on decent conditions.

One problem the planners had anticipated, on D-Day, was the risk of air collision. On D-Day, there would be literally hundreds of aircraft milling around in the skies of France, and it was far more likely that some would run into each other, than into the Luftwaffe. A hundred thousand gallons of whitewash and twenty thousand paint brushes were supplied to the Allied Airforce, and three broad white bands were painted on the wings and fuselage of every parachute aircraft and glider in the Allied command.

U.S. Airborne troopers during the flight.

Mass parachute drop of the U.S. Airborne.

The wind still seemed to be blowing strongly, far from the coast, at the North Witham airbase, near Nottingham, when the pathfinders of the 101st Division emplaned. The men were heavily loaded, carrying in addition to their normal equipment, the Eureka radio, beacons, lights and batteries. Some of the men had the additional task of reconnoitering routes from the drop zones to the various objectives, which would make for swift deployment when the main force arrived. One example will serve to set the tone for the whole night.

The pathfinders of the 502nd Regiment, had to find a route from their drop zone near Ste-Mere-Eglise to their Regimental task, a battery of coastal guns near UTAH, which they were to knock out before dawn. They took off at 22.00 hours on the night of 5th June and had a quiet, uneventful, flight to the west coast of the Cotentin. There, they ran into the first difficulty, for low cloud and fog prevented the pilots from spotting any positive spot on the ground to check their navigation on crossing the French Coast. They were dropped, therefore, two miles from their correct location, which was, under the circumstances, not too bad, and duly set up their equipment in open fields north of Ste-Mere-Eglise.

For the next two hours the pathfinders waited in the darkness, listening to bursts of machine gun fire and watching the odd flight of tracer as the now alert Germans began to investigate the appearance of groups of parachutists until, just after 1 a.m. the deep drone of hundreds of engines announced the arrival of the main force.

Aircraft seemed to be appearing over the drop zone from all points of the compass and as the 101st's pathfinders met the men now

landing, they were more than a little disconcerted to discover that the regiment now descending on their drop zone was the 505th Parachute Regiment of the 82nd Airborne Division. Something had gone seriously wrong.

It was the same story on almost all the other pathfinder marked drop zones, and many men were not descending on regular drop zones at all, but simply jumping blind into the night. The 101st, instead of landing in four tight groups, were scattered over 300 square miles of Normandy. Some landed over 30 miles from their correct drop zones. All over the Cotentin, chaos and bad luck, combined with bad management, confused the operation from the outset. Even the glider forces suffered. The great advantage of gliders, apart from their ability to lift heavy equipment, lay in the fact that they could put down men in organised groups. However, even here, things went wrong. The first glider down, carrying Brigadier General Platt, Assistant-Commander of the 101st, landed perfectly on a well marked landing zone. Unfortunately his glider ran across the marking lights, totally destroying them, and the other gliders, landing in the pitch dark, crashed, with heavy losses among the passengers and crew.

The more obvious landing zones had already been marked by the Germans who added to the confusion on the drop zones by mortar fire and machine gunning.

The experience of General Maxwell Taylor, who jumped at the head of his 101st Division, is typical of the experience of the main force parachutists on the night of 5th June. General Maxwell Taylor flew in the lead aircraft of his Division, on what would be his fifth jump. All the 101st drops were from aircraft of the 9th

An Allied Glider crash lands on D-Day.

Dead pilots beside their wrecked Horsa glider at Ste–Mere–Eglise.

U.S. Airforce Troop Carrier Squadron. On the way to France, the General slept on the floor of the aircraft, knowing he would need all the rest he could get later on. This feat was much admired by the other troopers in the aircraft. Once over the Cotentin coast, by which time the men were hooked up and at action stations, the 101st ran into considerable anti-aircraft fire from German positions along the coast. The aircraft pilots, naturally but unfortunately, took evasive action, junking and weaving about to shake off the anti-aircraft fire and searchlights.

This threw the standing paratroops off their feet, and into a tangle of men and equipment struggling on the floor of the aircraft. At such a time, a paratrooper has only one instinct to get out of this aircraft, with its crazy pilot, and into the safety of his parachute. As the red warning lights over the exit door changed to the green GO, the paratroopers didn't hesitate. As fast as they could, pushing the man in front, and ignoring the man behind, they flung themselves out into the skies of France.

Inevitably the drops were widely dispersed and as the men were often dropped too low, and at too great a speed, many were injured on landing. Broken limbs and even more severe injuries took a heavy toll of the Division even before they got out of their parachutes, and most were lost. On checking later, one group found that there had been a gap of four miles between the first man in their aircraft to jump and the last. One aircraft skirted the drop zone altogether, the green light never went on, and the pilot took his paratroopers back to England. What they did to him when they got there is not recorded.

Others were landed in the sea, or drowned, loaded down with their equipment in the flood waters of the Douve or the Merderet Rivers, and in those around Carentan. As the paratroopers landed, and in seeking and failing to find the other members of their aircraft, they must have wondered if Air Marshal Leigh Mallory's forebodings on their fate had not been all too accurate.

One who must certainly have thought so was General Maxwell Taylor, for on landing, he found himself not commanding 6,000 fighting men, but completely alone.

The bulk of his Division was dispersed over an area about ten miles square, generally south east of Ste-Mere-Eglise. A further thirty per cent of the Division were outside this area, and most of these were quickly rounded up by the Germans. General Taylor's first encounter in Normandy was with a solitary trooper from the 501st Regiment. They were so pleased to see each other that General and Private hugged each other with delight in the darkness. The General and his sole subordinate next encountered Brigadier General McAuliffe, who commanded the Divisional Artillery, and a war correspondent.

The first organised group he encountered was of the 3rd Battalion of the 501st, commanded by Lt. Colonel Ewell. Ewell had had an uneventful jump, although his battalion was widely scattered, and like everyone else, he didn't know where he was. It was not for some hours that they located their position near the church at Ste Marie du Mont. This was near one of the causeway exits from UTAH Beach, which was the objective of two battalions of the 506th Regiment.

However, since neither battalion had been dropped on the right spot, General Taylor

The heavy equipment comes in.

decided to lead his scratch formation to the attack, and capture the causeway exit. The two battalions would have had 1,200 men for the job. General Taylor's force consisted of the 40 available men of the 3rd Battalion of the 501st, and 45 members of the divisional staff, most of whom were officers.

The group contained two Generals, a Chief of Staff, two Colonels, a Major, several Captains and eight Lieutenants, and totalled in all eighty-five men. 'Never.' remarked General Taylor, wryly, 'have so few been commanded by so many.'

Lt. Col. Ewell was placed in command, and the force made their way, against light opposition, toward Pouppeville, collecting men as they went. By Pouppeville they had grown to about 150 men, from all regiments, and of both Divisions. The group had 18 casualties in the fight for Pouppeville, but they took the village, with 35 prisoners, and secured the landward exit of the causeway just after dawn. Coming slowly down the causeway towards them, was a tank, and taking no chances, the paratroopers greeted it with a burst of machine gun fire. It stopped, and displayed an orange identification panel and from the reeds on either side of the causeway rose infantry, also with yellow flags waving. They were from the 4th U.S. Infantry, coming from the sea.

All over the Cotentin, the paratroopers were in action. They might be dispersed, lost and confused, but they had weapons and ammunition, and they were determined to make a fight of it. They cut telephone wires, shot up patrols and ambushed roads. Slowly they coalesced into larger groups, and thus, fighting hard, they prevented the Germans grouping for a move against UTAH. In addition, one by one, using scratch forces like that accumulated by General Taylor and Lt. Col. Ewell they took their objectives.

One of these was Ste-Mere-Eglise, at about 4 a.m. on 6th June, which gained the distinction of being the first town in Normandy to be liberated by the Allies, falling to a depleted battalion of the 82nd Airborne.

Ste-Mere-Eglise had been having a disturbed night even before the invasion began. A fire had started in the main square, and called for the presence of the town fire brigade and the attention, as spectators, of most of the town's population.

Thus distracted, watching the flames light up the square and flicker the walls of the fine old church in the centre, they hardly heard the engines as the parachute aircraft arrived. It was the sight of descending parachutes, lit red from the fire, each with a dangling man, together with the sudden bursts of fire from the German garrison, that finally alerted the citizens to what was happening and drove them to cover.

It was another accident, the dropping of

The church in the main square, Ste-Mere-Eglise.

men on the town, and those who landed in the town paid for it with their lives. One actually fell into the fire, another was hooked by his parachute onto the church spire. Others landed in the trees around the square, or fell heavily onto the stones. All were shot down or quickly captured.

Apart from this, the 82nd had a generally better drop than the 101st. The leading regiment landed on the drop zone and by 4 a.m. had taken Ste-Mere-Eglise, and cut the Cherbourg-Carentan road. The two other regiments had a much worse time during the drop, and most of their heavy equipment went astray. The 82nd were supposed to land astride the River Merderet, and as the area around this river had been flooded, many men fell into floodwater, two to three feet deep. Under normal conditions a fit man could simply stand up, wet but unhurt, but if carrying up to 100 lbs of equipment and ammunition, and tugged over by the collapsing parachute, standing up was a task that some at least found too difficult and they therefore drowned.

The 82nd had one great advantage in that they were quickly able to find their position on the ground, for the Cherbourg-Carentan railway line on its embankment above the Merderet made a perfect landmark, and had therefore grouped into sufficient strength to disperse or repel any counter attack the Germans could make against them. The Germans in the Cotentin came from three infantry divisions, the 243rd, the 709th, and the 91st. The 91st had been specially trained in anti-invasion tactics, but the Commander of the 91st was ambushed and killed by the paratroopers of the 82nd Division during the night. Carentan was garrisoned by a German airborne unit, the 6th Parachute Regiment.

The German reaction to the paratroop landings was surprisingly slow. Had they reacted quicker, the two American Divisions might have been severely mauled. As it was, the paratroopers, facing up to the situation in which they found themselves, took the initiative, and held on to it. When the Germans realised what was happening, they found it difficult to mount a co-ordinated counter attack against the large but scattered force now harassing their positions. Communications began to break down as 'phone wires were cut; repair parties and despatch riders were ambushed; small patrols disappeared, and large ones were overwhelmed. Heavy fighting by Squads and Companies broke out all over the Cotentin, and this was fighting in which time was on the side of the Americans, for at dawn, the sea invasion must come, and they had already, by their activities made certain of its success.

After D-Day, when they re-assembled again in England, and counted the cost, it was seen that the American airborne divisions had suffered about twenty per cent casualties on D-Day, half of these killed or missing. This was bad, but nothing like as bad as the seventy per cent forecasted by Leigh Mallory. Only twenty parachute aircraft had been shot down out of eight hundred employed.

The paratroops did not take all their D-Day objectives. Carentan was not taken, and the bridges over the Douve were still held by the Germans. But they had given the 1st U.S. Army a foothold in France, and a bridgehead in the Cotentin, from which Cherbourg could be quickly reduced. Above all they assured the success of the landings on UTAH Beach. For 12,000 troopers, sorely harassed and scattered at the start, that is a considerable achievement.

General Gavin's foxhole, 6th June 1944.

THE RED DEVILS

'Le cheval volant, le Pegasus
qui a les narines de feu'!

'Gentlemen', said Brigadier Hill of 3rd Parachute Brigade, just before D-Day, 'do not be daunted if chaos reigns. It undoubtedly will.' There speaks the voice of experience. It is a sad fact, but true, that in war, in spite of the best plans and efforts of all concerned to prevent it, matters go rapidly awry from the moment the first shot is fired, and frequently before. It is, therefore, encouraging to note that many commanding officers were well aware of this fact, and advised their men accordingly. It is this facet of war that makes the study of military history so fascinating, for it is in the actual reaction of a General and his forces to events as they develop, that the stuff of history resides. Plans are fine, but as a rule they just don't work in any detail.

The Sixth Airborne Division which would land on the eastern flank of the Allied Liberation Army, was raised in England in the Spring of 1943. A year later, in the Spring of 1944, Sixth Airborne was commanded by Major General Sir Richard Gale, and consisted of the 3rd Parachute Brigade, the 5th Parachute Brigade and a glider formation, the 1st Airlanding Brigade. Allied glider

Waiting to jump.

formations at this time flew in three main types, the 'Horsa', a twenty-four seater, the 'Hamilcar', which could take forty, and the 'Waco' which was more popular with the Americans.

For the airborne operations of the day, the glider was essential. Only in gliders could guns, jeeps, scout cars, and heavy ammunition be transported. The glider needed no runway to land on, and was, on landing anyway, strictly expendable. They could stand up to very rough treatment, and needed skilled handling. The British gliders were piloted by men of the Glider Pilot Regiment, a regiment of Sergeants, each trained in infantry fighting, and ready, once he had deposited his passengers, to join in with them, in fighting the enemy.

Each Airborne division contained one airlanding brigade, consisting of three infantry battalions turned over to an airborne role. Indeed, at this time most British parachute units were not composed of pure volunteers, but were infantry units converted en bloc, to parachute troops. Any man could opt out, and transfer to a normal infantry unit, if

A Dakota tows off a D-Day glider.

parachute jumping was not to his taste, but the incidence of men doing this was surprisingly small.

The Sixth Airborne Division would be taken to Normandy by aircraft of 38 Group and 46 Group R.A.F. The task of the Division was to land on the high ground between the Rivers Orne and Dives, to secure the bridges over the former, and destroy those over the latter. The high ground was important as it overlooked the British invasion beaches along the Calvados coast, and indeed, contained German coastal artillery batteries. The bridges over the Orne, and the nearby Caen Canal, that links Caen with the sea, had to be captured before the Germans could destroy them, to give the invasion forces access to the high ground, while this flank could be effectively sealed off from counter attack if the Dives bridges were destroyed, especially since just across the Dives lay the formidable 21st Panzer Division, the one German armoured formation close to the invasion coast, and positioned to roll up the invasion

Pegasus Bridge, 6th June 1944, Major Howard's glider lies beyond the trees.

from the flank if given the chance to do so.

The task for Sixth Airborne therefore was a difficult and dangerous one, and exposed them to the almost certain attack from an armoured division, the type of attack that lightly equipped paratroopers are least able to deal with.

Most of the men in Sixth Airborne had not been in action before, and were as untried as the division itself. They had, however, been extensively trained for their tasks, and were confident in their ability to overcome any difficulty they might encounter. The first task, the securing of the bridges over the Orne and the Caen Canal was allocated to 5th Parachute Brigade, landing in the north of Ranville, and clear landing grounds for the advanced headquarters and anti-tank guns, that would arrive later by glider. For the actual capture of the bridges they had under command a glider force of 200 men from the 2nd Oxfordshire and Buckinghamshire Light Infantry, and The Royal Engineers, command by Major John Howard. This force would take

The first house, a bar, to be liberated by Sixth Airborne Division.

the bridges by coup-de-main, landing as close to them as possible, hoping to overwhelm the enemy before they had a chance to fire the demolition charges.

Major Howard's plan appeared to suffer a considerable setback when, as Rommel's efforts to defend Normandy developed, anti-invasion posts sprouted in the fields around the Orne and the Caen Canal bridges. However, when he showed the air photographs of these defences to his glider pilots they were not a bit disconcerted, as they considered that they could use the posts to run the glider wings against, and thus slow down their landing speed.

This is, in fact, just what happened, when just after midnight on 6th June, the gliders swooped to earth beside the enemy bridges. With a series of grinding snaps, Howard's glider ploughed through the posts and came to a halt barely fifty yards from the gaunt steel outline of the Canal Bridge. The other two gliders were close behind, and the defences were quickly overwhelmed, before the demolition charges, already in place could be fired. On the far side of the bridge was a small house. If Ste-Mere-Eglise was the first town to be liberated, Sixth Airborne can certainly claim to have liberated the first house, and were delighted to find that it was also a bar, serving, for a limited period, free champagne.

A mile away, the rest of Howard's force had a successful landing, and captured the bridge over the Orne. Both bridges were quickly cleared of their demolition charges and the 'Ox and Bucks' then dug in round their objectives to await reinforcements from the 5th Parachute Brigade, which was due to land near Ranville at 1 a.m.

Unfortunately — that word again — high winds carried 5th Parachute Brigade's pathfinders away from their drop zone and over to the east. With no time to march back, they set up their beacons where they were, with the result that the main force, also affected by the westerly winds, and their aircraft harassed by heavy anti-aircraft fire, went even further east, and were unable to get back to the bridges before German infantry, with armoured support, began to probe Howard's defences. The battalion detailed to reinforce Howard was widely scattered, and could muster only 200 men to support the defenders at the bridges, but this was just enough, for the moment, and as the night wore on, more paratroopers arrived, trickling in in small groups or alone, obeying the old military dictum of when in doubt, head for the sound of the gunfire.

The Germans, mainly from the 711th and 716th Infantry Divisions, and 21st Panzer, which had been on training manoeuvres around Caen, reacted quickly to the airborne landings, and sent out strong formations to seek out and destroy the paratroopers. There was, fortunately, a similar lack of co-ordination among the defenders, and no attempt was made to organise a proper sweep. This may well have been due to the absence from his headquarters of Field Marshal Rommel. It was his misfortune, that, on the two crisis moments of his career, at Alamein and D-Day, he should not be in a position to take a grip on his forces while events were still fluid, and ideally suited to Rommel's particular style of warfare.

Rommel, thinking the bad weather and Channel gales would prevent a landing, had taken the opportunity to make a swift visit to Germany. He would surely have grasped the significance of the airborne landings, and in

General Gale's glider.

particular the noticeable gap between them, along the Calvados Coast.

In his absence, the battle was conducted by local commanders, and their abilities were confused by the night, and the damage the paratroopers were doing to their communications. 5th Parachute Brigade had already seized the river crossings, and had now to proceed to their second task, the securing of the ground around them, at Ranville and Benouville. One hundred and thirty-five aircraft took 5th Parachute Brigade to their drop zones, and the Brigade suffered nearly one hundred casualties in the drop and had over four hundred missing when they assembled. Most of the missing trailed in later.

7th Battalion made immediately for the Orne and Caen Canal bridges. 13th Battalion began clearing the drop zone of obstacles ready for the arrival of the Airlanding Brigade, and cleared the enemy out of Ranville, while 12th Battalion, although fifty per cent under strength, made for their area, the high ground south of Ranville.

At three-thirty the Divisional Headquarters, with heavy equipment and anti-tank guns came in by glider bringing the Divisional Commander, Major General Gale. By dawn 5th Parachute Brigade were in position, and awaiting whatever the day would bring.

Brigadier Hill's 3rd Parachute Brigade was taken to Normandy by the 46 Group R.A.F. The Brigade had three main tasks. First, and most vital, was the elimination of the Merville Battery. Second, this accomplished, was the securing of the high ground at Le Plein, by the Canadian Parachute Battalion, and thirdly, they had to destroy the four bridges over the Dives, at Troan, Bures, Robehomme and Varaville. Having achieved all this the Brigade was to concentrate in the area of the Bois de Bavant.

The Merville Battery lies among farmland on high ground south of Franceville Plage. The concrete casements, feet thick, enclosed heavy artillery pieces, and a garrison of 200 men entrenched to defend the guns. These were protected by minefields, barbed wire, and fixed line machine guns, and their living quarters were underground, with concrete head cover against bombing. The heavy guns of the Merville Battery could fire right down the British beaches across the Orne, and it was vital that the battery be eliminated by first light. The task was given to Lt. Colonel Otway, and the 9th Parachute Battalion. Otway found an area, near Newbury in Berkshire, that resembled Merville, and having had the landscape bulldozed into the appropriate contours, practised his battalion endlessly in the assault. The plan was that the battery would be bombed by a Lancaster force, just before the assault, and then, the minefields having been gapped by sappers, the battery would be attacked by the entire battalion. As they arrived, another force, in three gliders, would crash land right onto the battery position. Finally, if all else failed, the battery would be engaged by the guns of the Fleet. This was a fine, if complicated plan, and went wrong from the start.

9th Battalion had a terrible drop, across the valley of the Dives, and many men were drowned in the floods and swamps. One group landed thirty miles from their proper drop zone, while Otway landed right by a

The casements of the Merville Battery today.

A memorial at Pegasus Bridge.

German Headquarters, and was almost captured while still in his parachute. When he reached the battalion rendezvous he found he had only 150 men, and none of the special equipment he needed.

As with the Americans on the other side of the coast, Otway nevertheless went ahead with what he had, finding, on arriving at the assembly area near the battery, that some of his men had already arrived and had cleared a few tracks through the minefields, digging up mines in the dark with their bayonets. Otherwise all was chaos. The bombers dropped their loads a mile away, and the gliders crashed, failing to find their objective in the dark. Otway led his men into the minefields, and they took the Merville Battery by storm, capturing thirty of the garrison and killing the rest. By dawn, they had destroyed the guns and gathering their scattered men as they went, were on their way to the consolidation area.

The bridges over the Dives were successfully blown, and 3rd Parachute Brigade had, like the 5th, secured all their objectives by first light. In the early afternoon of D-Day Major Howard's men, by the bridges at Benouville, heard the pipes, as Lord Lovat's personal piper led the 1st S.S. (Commando) Brigade across the Canal Bridge to join them.

Throughout D-Day, 6th Airborne beat off an ever heavier series of attacks by the Germans. Luckily, the Division had by now most of the heavy equipment, and with their anti-tank guns, and some help from Naval gunfire, they were able to hold on, and improve their defences, until joined in the late afternoon by two battalions of 1st Airlanding Brigade, and in the evening by seaborne troops from the 3rd Infantry Division, to secure their flanks.

On the evening of D-Day General Gale had under command, six parachute battalions, two commando units, two airlanding battalions, some light tanks and fifty anti-tank guns.

The Division had had a hard time and there would be harder times ahead. The Division, new to war, was to suffer 4,500 casualties in Normandy, but the eastern open flank of the invasion was secure.

Digging in.

A beachhead on Utah Beach.

UTAH

'A very little little let us do,
And all is done.'

UTAH Beach, some ten miles long, lies on the coast of the Cotentin, east of Ste-Mere-Eglise, and is a smoothly shelving, open beach of compact grey sand, firm, and free from natural obstacles. In the rear of the beach are sand dunes up to 20 feet high and a low sea wall, which carries a narrow coast road. Behind this the land is low lying, and marshy, and in 1944 had been flooded and mined to a depth of two miles inland, as part of Rommel's anti-invasion preparations. Passage across this marsh depended on narrow causeways which in peaceful times give the villagers access to the beach. There were five of these, leading from the south to Pouppeville, Houdienville, Audouville, St. Martin de Varreville, and Ste Germain.

The inland exits from these causeways were to be seized by the airborne forces and it was anticipated that if they did their work well, the beach defences could be quickly overwhelmed and the Americans rapidly debouch across the Peninsula as a step towards the capture of Cherbourg.

The assault on UTAH was to be made by the 4th Infantry Division of Major General J. L. Collins' VII Corps. Collins was one of the youngest Major-Generals in the American army and a man of considerable energy and ingenuity. Prior to his appointment in Europe, he had been a successful Divisional Commander in the Pacific, serving with distinction in the campaign on Guadalcanal. His experience there was to stand him in good stead, during the fighting in the Normandy bocage. Many allied Commanders found the close banks and hedgerows of the bocage unduly constricting to their tactical plans, and their advance slowed accordingly. Collins, after the jungle, found the bocage positively roomy, and accordingly sent his Corps

travelling up to Cherbourg in record time.

But all that lay in the future, on the Sixth of June.

VII Corps, which formed part of General Omar Bradley's 1st Army, was to land on UTAH at 0630 hours, half tide, on D-Day. The assault formation, 4th Infantry Division, would be supported by 32 D-D tanks and a small amount of specialised equipment, mainly bulldozers, to clear the beach obstructions and deal with the beach defences. The Americans would be opposed by the German 729th and 919th Divisions, which with a division of disaffected Russian Georgian troops, were positioned directly on the coast.

Behind them were two infantry divisions, the 709th and 243rd, both of which were composed largely of 'stomach' battalions, infantry considered fit only for coastal defence work. There seemed to be no insurmountable problem here, but early in June, Intelligence reported that the formidable 91st Division had arrived in the area and the possibility of some tough opposition grew stronger. 91st Division had been specially trained in anti-invasion work, but suffered a major setback early on, when their Divisional Commander, returning from a map exercise on the night of D-Day, was ambushed and killed by American paratroopers.

The VII Corps plan called for the cutting of the peninsula at the base, before turning north to take Cherbourg. Their landing, preceded by the airborne attack, would be supported by heavy bombers, drenching Naval gun fire and rockets on the beach and D-D tanks for close support. 4th Division would be reinforced for the landing with various special groups, notably extra artillery and anti-tank

Sherman tank on Utah Beach.

units, and a detachment of 4th Cavalry, to capture the Iles de Marcouf, which lay off the assault beach. This assault force was to sail to the landing in 865 assorted vessels in twelve convoys, under the command of Rear Admiral Don P. Moon, U.S.N.

Moon's task force arrived at their assembly point off UTAH at 0200 hours in the dark morning of 6th June. The passage from England over a stormy heaving sea had been a considerable opening nightmare for the troops on board. The gale's temporary abatement may have been noticeable to experienced seamen, but to the infantry crammed in their troop-decks, with nothing to do but wait and vomit, it seemed terrible, and, in spite of what may have been awaiting them, many wished only to get ashore and have firm ground under their feet again. The first ashore were 124 men of the 4th Cavalry, who landed on the offshore Iles de Marcouf, which were found deserted. Meanwhile, as the troops transhipped into their landing craft, 247 Marauders of the 9th U.S. Airforce, began to bomb the beach, as from offshore, the warships of Task Force 125 began to fire on the shore batteries.

The movement ashore of the assault craft was supported by 33 rocket and gun ships, to give close support to the landing. The D-D tanks were launched 3,000 yards from the beach, and 28 out of 32 made it ashore. The first infantry wave, of the 8th Infantry 2nd Battalion in 20 LCVP's got ashore unopposed, and highly delighted, waving their rifles in the air and cheering as they ran across the beach towards the dunes. They had not reached them, however, when it became clear that they had landed in the wrong place.

Once again something had gone wrong.

2nd Battalion should have landed opposite Exit 3, which led to Audouville. They landed over a mile south, opposite Exit 1, leading to Pouppeville. It seems that one of the control vessels, which should have led them in, had been lost, and the strong set of the incoming tide had carried them off course. This initial error could have been disastrous. Luckily, in the first wave was the Assistant Commander of the 4th Infantry Division, Brigadier General Theodore Roosevelt Jnr. General Roosevelt was one of the U.S. Army's great characters, and although 57 years old at the time, he had persuaded his Divisional Commander to let him go ashore in the first wave.

This proved providential, for General Roosevelt knew what to do, and had the authority to make his decision stick. He signalled to the following waves to ignore their original headings and follow in behind the initial wave. He then walked up and down the foreshore, cheering the men ashore, regardless of the machine fire beginning to sweep the beach. General Roosevelt died of a heart attack two weeks after the landings but his action on D-Day won him the Congressional Medal of Honour.

Quite apart from avoiding disastrous confusion, the defences to the south of UTAH were less strong than those in front of their original landing place, and more easily overcome. The beach obstacles consisted of three lines of obstructions, mainly steel pikes, posts crowned with fused Teller mines, steel caltrops, tetrahedra and hedgehogs. All were mined. The initial plan called for the combat engineers to clear a number of 50 yard gaps in these obstacles to let landing craft in when the tide rose.

There was no specialised armour, and the obstacles had to be blown by combat engineers, and then cleared away by bull-dozers. The engineers also had to blow gaps in the sea wall, and clear the beach exits to the causeways. The entire beach was cleared in an hour, at a cost in killed and injured of only 45 men. Opposition on the beach was fortunately light — fortunately, because during the hour it took to clear the beach and let the traffic off, the tanks and vehicles began to assemble in a manner that would have provided sitting targets for enfilading artillery had there been any. In the main, opposition came from indirect artillery fire from inland batteries, and mortars.

The German infantry manning the coastal positions had been shocked and dazed by the bombing and rocket fire, and startled by the sight of the D-D tanks rearing dripping out of the waves. Coastal strong points were reduced by the 3rd Battalion, 2nd Infantry Regiment, and as more men came ashore, the chief problem on the beachhead became traffic congestion. Owing to the southward swing of the landings, only Exit 2 could be

A memorial behind the guns on Utah.

used by the vehicles, and this was mined, and defended by pillboxes. Behind the beach, however, the fighting intensified, both along the causeways and across the flooded fields.

By 10 a.m. the seaborne forces were pushing inland hard, pulled on by the sounds of firing up ahead, where the scattered groups of paratroops were striving to keep the exits clear. The first assault formation, 2nd Battalion, 8th Infantry Regiment, was heading for Pouppeville, harassed all the way by small arms fire. On the way they found and recruited a D-D tank, which led their advance along the causeway. At the far end they were met with a hail of fire, which forced the tank to halt and the infantry to take cover in the water. The fire sounded familiar, and stopped when recognition flags were displayed, as down the causeway to meet them came the men of the 101st Airborne.

By the evening of D-Day, 4th Infantry Division were well ashore, and linking up with the paratroopers all along their Divisional front. They had had only 197 casualties during the day, and this included 60 men lost

U.S. Rangers clean weapons before the attack on Pointe du Hoc.

at sea. Moreover the landings had proceeded smoothly and at great speed, uninterrupted by any interference from German aircraft, ships or coastal artillery.

The Luftwaffe made only six sorties over the beachhead on D-Day, and these were driven off by the hundreds of Allied fighters. German Naval craft from Le Havre succeeded in sinking only one ship, the Norwegian destroyer 'Svenner'; Admiral Moon of UTAH, lost the destroyer 'Corry' to a mine, plus a patrol craft and four landing craft. The UTAH assembly area was, moreover, spared the

attentions of the most formidable battery on the Normandy coast, the 155mm guns on the Pointe du Hoc.

The Pointe du Hoc juts into the Bay of the Seine, on the Calvados coast, east of the Cotentin, and overlooked the assembly areas for the UTAH and OMAHA shipping.

On cliffs 100 feet above the sea, the six heavy guns on the battery could engage any ships within fifteen miles, and it was vital that the battery be destroyed before dawn on D-Day. This task was entrusted to Lt. Col.

James E. Rudder, commanding the Provisional Ranger Force drawn from the 2nd and 5th Battalions United States Rangers which were the American equivalent of the British Commandos.

Raised in 1942, they had been in action in North Africa, and Italy, where they had gained a formidable reputation in the fighting at Salerno. The attack on the battery at Pointe du Hoc would be a classic raiding task, and was an ideal task for special service troops, provided they could pull it off. The cliffs at Pointe du Hoc rear up sheer out of the sea for 100 feet, and the cliff face had been laced with barbed wire and trip flares. The battery was right on the cliff edge, and the outer casements were regularly patrolled. There would be little chance of a quiet approach and Rudder decided to storm up the cliff, getting his men up fast with the use of scaling ladders and ropes on grapples fired from mortars. He trained his men in these techniques on the high chalk cliffs of the Isle of Wight, and on D-1 the force in L.C.A's lay off Pointe du Hoc waiting for moonrise. The assault craft were detected during the run in, and bombarded by shore artillery. An air strike, planned to cover their landing, succeeded only in depositing rubble at the base of the cliff, which made the landing difficult, and most of the mortar grapnels fell short. To add to their problems, the Germans above were alert, and tossed grenades down on the Rangers, as they strove to climb the cliffs.

At this critical point, the destroyer accompanying the L.C.A's came to their assistance, closing in shore, and strafing the cliff top with her secondary armament.

Thus encouraged, the mortar crews tried again, successfully this time, and the Rangers swarmed up the ropes, overrunning the battery position, only to find to their chargrin, that the casements were empty.

The guns were missing, and the Rangers sent out patrols which located them in an orchard half a mile inland, where they were destroyed. Enemy reinforcements were already moving in to counter attack, and Rudder's men dug in to hold them off. The remnants of the Provisional Ranger Force were still fighting when reinforcements from the main landing on OMAHA broke through to relieve them two days later.

Off Pointe du Hoc, General Omar Bradley awaited news of the landings aboard the U.S.S. Augusta. By 10 a.m. his worries were deepening. He had heard good news from UTAH where the landings were going well, and this indicated also that the Airborne units had succeeded in their task. From the Rangers he had heard nothing but, on the other hand, the absence of artillery fire from the Pointe du Hoc battery seemed to indicate that matters there had gone according to plan.

From OMAHA, however, the news was ominous. Since dawn Bradley had received a series of disconnected reports and messages, recounting a tale of sinkings, heavy artillery fire, chaos and casualties. At 10 a.m. Bradley received his first report from the Corps Commander for OMAHA Beach, General Gerow. It reported the loss of most of the D-D tanks, heavy machine gun fire on an obstacle encrusted beach, and a rumour tht the assault waves were pinned down in the surf, unable to move.

The day at OMAHA was not going well for the Allies, and at mid-morning bore every sign of a major reverse.

BLOODY OMAHA

'God of Battles, steel my
Soldiers hearts.'

Every battle involves at least one pounding match, where fine plans and tactics seem to dissolve into sheer murderous fighting. Even as he read the reports from UTAH, General Bradley must have reflected that things seemed to be going too well for him, and the news from OMAHA could have been no surprise. It was to be expected that there would be a major setback somewhere.

OMAHA Beach is a wide gently curving beach, about four miles long, in the only gap in the cliffs that run from the Pointe du Hoc towards Port en Bessin. It was an obvious point for a landing, and the German defences were more developed here than at many other points along the coast.

The defences at OMAHA were also helped by the nature of the terrain. The beach shelves gently, leading up to a high shingle bank, along the top of which runs a road, resting on the sea wall. Behind the road is a shallow belt of sand, leading to high dunes which provide visibility over the entire landing area.

There are only four exits off the beach, and these were protected by 35 pillboxes, 8

concrete bunkers with 75mm guns, and 85 machine gun posts. The heavy guns in concrete emplacements were sited to enfilade the beach, the concrete on the seaward side being strong enough to withstand direct hits from heavy Naval guns.

Along OMAHA the Germans had mustered in addition, 18 anti-tank positions, mounting guns of between 37mm and 75mm, 6 Nebelwerfer (multiple barrelled mortar) pits, 38 rocket batteries and 4 field artillery positions.

The beach could therefore be swept with fire from end to end, by mortars and machine guns on the heights at either end, or dug in in the woods behind the beach area. In addition to weaponry, the Germans had added to the beach's natural strength with a range of obstacles. There were three rows of these below the high water mark. There were mines and barbed wire along the shingle bank, and in the strip between the bank and the dunes. All in all OMAHA was the most formidable position along the Normandy coast, and it would take good luck and good management to overcome it. Neither was in adequate

Bloody shambles under fire on Omaha beach.

Omaha today.

supply. The assault division for OMAHA was the U.S. 1st Infantry Division, known as 'The Big Red One', the most famous and most experienced American Division in Europe, veteran of North Africa, Sicily and Italy.

During these early campaigns 1st Infantry Division had established a great reputation in combat with the enemy at the front, and an even greater one for combat with the military police in the rear areas. General Bradley recalls in his Memoirs that the 1st Infantry Division left a trail of looted bars and outraged mayors all the way from Arzew to Catania.

After the conclusion of the Sicilian campaign Bradley decided that the time had come to find a new Commander for 'The Big Red One', and found just the man he wanted in Major General Clarence R. Huebner, by repute the fiercest disciplinarian in the U.S. Army. Huebner had enlisted as a Private in 1910, and had already served in the 1st Infantry Division in every rank from Private to Colonel. He was not impressed by brawling in the streets, and if he admired 1st Infantry's battlefield performance, and admirable it certainly was, he kept it to himself. On his first day in command, he ordered a spit and polish full dress parade, and instituted a training programme which included the general officers universal cure-all for undisciplined units, lavish amounts of close order drill. The veterans of 1st Infantry ground their teeth, and muttered under their breath, but Huebner knew what he was doing, and wasn't worried about his popularity. His efforts to restore discipline saved lives and won a battle a year later on the coast of France, when 1st Infantry Division led Gerows V Corps to the Normandy assault. Close behind came another excellent Division from the same Corps, the 29th Infantry Division.

Basically the defences at OMAHA were too strong for the forces sent against them. The first wave consisted of 1,450 infantry men supported by 32 D-D tanks.

Their troubles began at the assembly point. Anticipating battery fire the infantry went down into their L.C.A's, and the D-D tanks from the L.S.T's were launched 12 miles from the beach. Out there, in the middle of the great bay, there was none of the protection that the Cotentin Peninsula offered to the craft off UTAH. The seas were rough, and many craft were swamped during the run in. Most of the infantry were racked with sea sickness, and the canvas screens of the D-D tanks were never designed to stand up to such seas for any length of time. Twenty-seven of the tanks foundered, drowning most of their crews, before the beach was reached.

On the beach the gale had piled up the seas, so that most of the obstacles were still covered. Finally the wind and tide together set up currents which carried many of the assault craft away from their designated areas, and it was a seasick, under-strength, unsupported and disorganised wave of infantry that finally got ashore.

The underwater obstacles immediately took their toll, sinking craft and blowing crews and occupants sky high, while from their vantage points on shore, the Germans flailed them with fire. Within minutes the assault was halted on the water's edge, taking heavy casualties and unable to hit back.

To trace the cause of this state of affairs one must go back to the original plan, in which too much was left to the infantry and too little use was made of the facilities available to support them. The pre-assault air strikes and Naval bombardments were too light, and too short, and in the event missed most of their targets. Even the rocket craft failed to strike the beach defences adequately. The landings at half tide, were upset by the weather, but as the tide was making, it was vital to clear the beach obstacles before the waves covered them, so that the big landing ships could bring in more guns and tanks to secure the foothold. The Americans would have found this task much easier had they taken the specialised armour offered by the British.

However, for reasons already explained, Bradley rejected this, and the task of clearing away the obstacles on fire-swept OMAHA was left to unprotected engineers of the U.S. Army's demolition teams. They didn't have a chance. Not only were their casualties appalling, but most of their equipment was lost on the run-in. A shell exploded the demolition charges one team was bringing ashore, and blew every man to pieces. Other engineers, working in the open were picked off by snipers or cut down by the machine guns. When they could attach charges to obstacles they had to kick the men hiding under them away before they could blow them up.

For hours the pitiless hail of enemy fire went on until OMAHA beach was a shambles of dead men, burning tanks and vehicles and wrecked landing craft. Out at sea, only fragments of this story were getting back, and more and more men were coming ashore, adding to the carnage and confusion on the beach. Some men managed to get across the beach and took shelter in the cover of the shingle bank. Here, in the few yards hard up against the shingle, they were comparatively safe from all but mortar and shell fire. As the morning wore on more men arrived, wet, exhausted, frequently without equipment or weapons. Many were wounded, and they were the lucky ones. The wounded left out on the open beach were drowned as the tide came in, bringing with it the men who had been sheltering on the waterline, and now came crawling up the beach with only their heads exposed above the waves. Even these were sniped by Germans from posts above the beachhead.

At 11 a.m. Bradley sent a Staff Officer ashore in a P.T. boat to examine the situation. He returned an hour later soaking wet, to report landing craft milling about in confusion, chased by shell fire, and 1st Infantry pinned against the sea wall. Only in one section, EASY RED, had the beach obstacles been cleared and craft making for this area to unload were creating a monster traffic jam that provided wonderful targets for the German artillery.

At noon, with the situation still critical, Bradley contemplated switching his follow-up forces to UTAH or the British beaches and was about to order the evacuation of OMAHA when he received a message from V Corps. 'Troops formerly pinned down on beaches now advancing up heights behind'.

Many factors had combined to halt the American assault at OMAHA. Others combined to get it started again, but the main ingredient that turned disaster into success, was simple human courage. Soldiers have to have many qualities in war, and endurance is probably the most vital. 'The Big Red One' and 29th Infantry endured much on OMAHA. A soldier needs discipline, and it was discipline that led the infantry, often just Privates or junior non-commissioned officers, to organise themselves, to hunt for weapons, to clean those they had of sand and sea water, and start to think of their situation and how they might get out of it.

It takes courage to move out even from behind the comparative safety of a bullet-swept wall, into the open, but all along that beach men, after hours of endurance, found the courage to do it. The advance seems to have begun again in several places all at about the same time. In one place an Officer led a sudden rush over the shingle bank, and found that the maching-gunning on the far side was less intense and movement possible. An Engineer Sergeant moved up and down, collecting explosives until he had enough to blow a hole in the sea wall, and this let other troops through. In some places men who had simply had enough, decided it was time to hit back, and stood up and walked across the shingle wall. They gapped the minefields by hand, losing men all the way, but slowly, painfully, the 1st Infantry Division began to get off the beach.

As at UTAH, there were general Officers

German infantry trenches above Omaha.

ashore, notably Colonel Taylor of the 1st Division who coined the immortal phrase, 'Two kinds of people are staying on this beach, the dead, and those that are going to die. Now let's get the hell out of here'. These men, and hundreds more saved the situation at OMAHA. So too did the discipline that General Heubner had drilled back into the 1st Infantry Division, a year before.

On the right of 1st Infantry Division, the 29th Infantry Division had come ashore opposite Vierville, and taken another thrashing from the enemy guns. There again, an Officer was around to point the way with his cry, 'They're murdering us here. Let's move inland and get murdered.'

'Get inland' was the watchword that set the beach alight. Scores of men were now on their feet and crossing the sea wall.

Offshore, once the situation became clear, General Heubner had acted fast to help his beleaguered Division. He called for Naval help, and destroyers were sent in close to the shore, engaging the German emplacements over open sights, and he stopped the rear-echelon support troops landing, sending instead more infantry and engineers to help the men ashore. Thanks to him, the Commanders ashore, and the courage of countless individuals, the assault began to move forward again. In little groups and companies, the Americans began to infiltrate the enemy defences, to take them in the rear and, one by one, to eliminate them. There was bitter fighting by 1st and 29th Infantry Divisions on the heights behind OMAHA, but by mid-afternoon the advance inland had begun.

The enemy resistance at OMAHA came as an unpleasant shock to the American command who had disregarded reports that the Wehrmacht's tough 352nd Infantry Regiment had taken over this sector of the coast, for the Americans expected to encounter the usual second rank troops. 352nd Division had only recently arrived in Normandy, but as battle trained troops they contested every step of the landing, reporting back to Rundstedt that they had thrown the invaders back into the sea. However, even as they were making this report, in the early afternoon, the balance was slowly tilting in the American's favour. The point of their spearhead may have been blunted, but there was a lot of weight behind the shaft and remorseless pressure together with the Naval gunfire and the constant arrival of fresh troops, gradually wore the Germans down. In mid-afternoon the situation seemed to warrant a close inspection, and General Bradley again sent a Staff Officer ashore to check on the troops progress and requirements.

He reported back with a story of a beach strewn with bodies and wreckage, but with the men ashore fighting their way inland. The most pressing need was for artillery and bulldozers. Sixteen bulldozers had been sent ashore during the morning. Only six reached OMAHA, and these were instantly destroyed by artillery fire. More were urgently needed to clear away the beach obstacles and push a path for tanks through the shingle bank and across the dunes. What good use the Americans could have made of specialised armour that morning, to clear the mines, silence the machine guns, breach the walls and give them support to get moving off that bloody ground. This is not hind-sight. The need for such devices had been proved at Dieppe and the armour existed and was available. However, every nation must fight its wars in its own way. General Bradley thought he could breach OMAHA with the courage of his infantry and luckily they had the courage to do it. It cost 1,000 of them their lives.

General Gerow, Commander of the V Corps went ashore at 7.30 p.m. on the evening of 6th June and set up his headquarters near Colleville. General Heubner found the atmosphere warmer when he joined the forward elements of his 1st Infantry Division, while on the right, the 29th Division were pushing hard towards Pointe du Hoc, to relieve the Rangers. Behind them, on the beach, the tide was going out, uncovering the dead, and an immense litter of equipment. Reinforcements were coming ashore, awed by the evidence of carnage all about them. They made their way slowly along the taped gaps in the minefields, past the blackened emplacements of the Atlantic Wall and their dead defenders. It had been a hard day on OMAHA Beach.

The sea wall Omaha Beach.

View of the sea from German casements on Pointe du Hoc.

THE BRITISH AND CANADIAN BEACHES

'Then forth, dear countrymen,
We doubt not of a fair and lucky war.
Cheerily to sea, the signs of war advance!

Under fire off Sword beach.

An hour after the American landings the British and Canadian Armies began to land on their beaches to the East. This time difference was due to the tides, which ebbed and flowed an hour later on the eastern end of the Calvados coast, and although the British were supposed, like the Americans, to land at half tide, they found that the gales in the Channel, combined with the prevailing westerly wind and tide set, had caused the water to pile up over the waiting beach obstacles and on the deployment area of the beach itself. Neverthe-

less, the British got off to a good start. The bombardment by Admiral Vian's Fleet lasted longer than that of the Americans, was made from closer in, and was correspondingly more accurate. The beaches were well marked, notably by the crews of the midget submarines X20 and X23, who came gasping to the surface, after a submersion that had lasted a whole day longer than they had expected. The D-D tanks were launched from close inshore, and most of the landing craft hit the right beach at the right time.

A Firefly tank comes ashore.

The troops themselves, although no less seasick than their American comrades, were in a notably good mood. Music blasted from loudspeakers on the troopships, bugles saluted one another from the packed landing craft, carrying men of the infantry battalions, and pipes blared away on craft taking the Highlanders ashore.

Once ashore, though, the resistance from the Germans was as fierce as anywhere along the coast. Moreover, the coast where the British and Canadians were to land, was fairly

well built up, and street fighting, which uses up infantry fast, began as soon as the beach was cleared.

The right hand troops of the British 2nd Army were from the 50th (Northumbrian) Division of XXX Corps. Their task was to penetrate the German defences on GOLD Beach between La Riviere and Le Hamel, and press on inland to take Bayeux. They had also, as a step towards establishing the British Mulberry Harbour, to take the small port of Arromanches. The Germans defending this

Troops of 50th Division come ashore.

sector came from the 352nd Division that was also at this time hammering the Americans at OMAHA.

H-Hour for 50th Division was 0725, and preceded by a strong Naval bombardment, the troops touched down dead on time. Owing to rough seas, it was decided not to launch the D-D tanks, but to beach the L.S.T's that carried them and land the tanks directly on the beach, which meant that they arrived after the infantry and not alongside them. Two brigades, the 231st and 69th formed the initial assault waves, the former at Le Hamel, and the latter at La Riviere. The 1st Hampshires were the right hand battalion of 231st Brigade, and were supposed to land at Le Hamel, and work along the coast to the west, taking Asnelles sur Mer, Arromanches, Tracy sur Mer, and Monvieux.

They landed in the face of heavy machine gun and artillery fire, and were soon entangled in minefields. It was 0900 hours before two companies were able to get off the beach and attack the pillboxes and machine gun posts from behind. But for the support of specialised armour, notably A.V.R.E's, firing petards against the pillboxes, they might not have got off the beach at all. It was not until the evening that Le Hamel and Arromanches finally fell, by which time the 1st Hampshires had sustained heavy casualties including the deaths of the C.O. and Second in Command, and a high proportion of the Company's Officers and men. On the left of the Hampshires, the 1st Dorsets and 2nd Devons got ashore, and with support from tanks of the Sherwood Rangers and 90th Field Regiment R.A. took the features on the high ground behind the coast towards Bayeux. Two hours behind the initial assault wave No.47 (Royal Marine) Commando came ashore.

47 had the task of capturing Port en Bessin, a small port which formed the right hand boundary of the 2nd British Army. Port en Bessin nestles in a hollow between cliffs about 150 feet high and is overlooked by high ground inland. It was defended by at least a company of German infantry, plus Naval personnel, entrenched in pillboxes over-looking the town and in strong points within the town itself. It was decided to take Port en Bessin from inland, which meant that 47 Commando had a march of ten miles through enemy territory before they even got to the assault area.

Their troubles, however, began on the run in to the beaches. Three L.C.A's were sunk on the run in, and on landing at Le Hamel, which should by then have been quiet, the Commando found the 1st Hampshires still fighting for a foothold. The Commando found their intended assembly area held by a company of Germans and suffered 40 casualties before they cleared them out of it.

They did, however, take 60 prisoners here, whose weapons served to re-equip those men from the sunk L.C.A's who had had to abandon their own equipment to swim ashore. It was nightfall before the depleted 47 Commando reached Port en Bessin, which they attacked at dawn. It took a further day of fighting before 47 took the town. They suffered over 200 casualties, some fifty per cent of their strength, but took their objective, and 300 prisoners in the process.

East of Le Hamel, the 69th Brigade landed at La Riviere, led by the 5th East Yorks., and the 6th Green Howards. The East Yorks. crossed the beach under heavy enfilade fire, and advanced inland through minefields to the German battery at Mont Fleury. However, one of their companies, on the side nearest La Riviere, was stopped on the beach, and was again saved from extinction by good tactics and the specialised armour. 79th Division, the 'Funnies', were in action that day all along the coast, manning their peculiar vehicles in support of the landing. They never fought as a Division, but, in a hundred small groups, they were punching holes in the Atlantic Wall. The fight of the East Yorks. and the 'Funnies' at La Riviere, is typical of these coastal actions.

At the western edge of La Riviere, an 88mm gun, protected as usual by reinforced concrete on the seaward side, had a field of fire right down the beach, and was covered from infantry attack by machine guns. The 88 and the machine guns opened up on the infantry L.C.A's as they beached, and the men waded ashore. More fire came from houses in the village itself, and some L.C.A's were spiked or blown up on the beach obstacles, killing or maiming passengers and crew. Two A.V.R.E. petard tanks were hit immediately they came ashore and blew up

Commandos land.

with a mighty roar covering the infantry with a shower of debris and under this and a hail of fire, the survivors of the company had to crouch for shelter under the sea wall. Here they were joined by the reserve company, also harassed on landing by machine gun and mortar fire. Help, however, was at hand. A D-D tank came along the beach to engage the machine guns, and under cover of the tank's guns, two platoons crossed the wall and began to wipe out the machine gun nests. A.V.R.E's and D-D's forced a passage through the sea

wall and La Riviere was captured by 0900 hours.

The 6th Green Howards captured the high ground near Creully, and the 5th East Yorks advanced through them to the banks of the River Seuelles, flushing out Germans from the cornfields as they advanced. Their reserve battalion, the 7th Green Howards, were now ashore, and the brigade was now advancing and by evening had covered seven miles inland. 69th Brigade also gained one of the first V.C's awarded in Normandy, won by

Beach control party take it easy.

C.S.M. Hollis of the Green Howards. During the course of the day, Hollis knocked out a pillbox, cleared German infantry firing from a trench, silenced a field gun with a Piat, and rescued two men under heavy fire, altogether a full day's work.

By nightfall, GOLD Beach was secure, and 50th Division was well inshore, and had linked up with the Canadians on their left, who had come ashore on JUNO.

Juno Beach came within the province of the British 1st Corps, and was assigned to the 3rd Canadian Division, supported by the 2nd Canadian Armoured Brigade. The Canadians had to breach the defences on JUNO, an open beach which lay astride the outfall of the River Seuelles and was backed by the towns of Courseulles and Bernieres. This done, they were to advance inland and capture Carpiquet aerodrome, on the outskirts of Caen.

It was anticipated that this would be a formidable task, for Caen was clearly the key to the German defences on the Normandy coast, and was defended by 21st Panzer and

Tank of the Royal Marine Support Regt.

716th Infantry Division. Montgomery intended to capture Caen at the first rush, hopefully before the defences were properly organised, and the instructions to General Crocker of 1st Corps were that Caen must be either captured or 'effectively masked' — i.e., neutralised, by the evening of D-Day. In particular he had to capture the big airfield at Carpiquet. If anyone could do this it would be the Canadians, who had great dash in the attack, and had besides, the score of Dieppe to pay off.

In spite of this, the Canadian assault got off to a bad start. Bad weather delayed the landing craft, and the obstacles were covered by the tide before the craft reached the beach. Many craft were blown up and others capsized or crashed on to the shore. The beach at high tide was too narrow to let the men and their tanks and vehicles get organised, and an immense traffic jam pounded by artillery and racked by machine gun fire soon built up, on the narrow sand strip above the water-line.

The Naval and air bombardment had failed to knock out the beach defences and the Canadian infantry suffered heavy casualties just getting off the beach. At Bernieres the Queen's Own Rifles of Canada had a bad time on landing, and only cleared the beach with the help of D-D tanks and Flails so that when the reserve battalion, the French-Canadian Regiment de la Chaundiere, came ashore half an hour later, they found the beach still under fire and strewn with dead, wounded and wreckage of landing craft and vehicles.

At Corseulles, the Royal Winnipeg Rifles and Regina Rifles made good progress, and by mid-afternoon the Canadian armour had cut the Caen-Bayeux road, having made a speedy advance inland of more than seven miles.

Before this could be exploited, and the Canadians push on to Caen, the Germans counter-attacked. The Canadian 8th Brigade in Bernieres met heavy opposition from Germans at Beny. It took a full scale attack by the Regiment de La Chaundiere to overcome them, and the effort delayed the 8th Brigade in their efforts to get forward. Caen did not fall on D-Day, or the next day. Not until the 10th July, by which time the town had been almost totally destroyed, did British and Canadian troops enter Caen.

However, the Canadians did advance further inland than any other troops on D-Day, threatening Caen and linking up later that day with 50th Division, to give the Allies a beachhead in the east 15 miles long and up to 7 miles deep.

Only on their left was there a failure, and this was produced by a classic combination of circumstances, which, better than any other, illustrates the fog of battle on D-Day.

Between 1st Corp's western beach, JUNO,

Canadian memorial at Bernieres.

German prisoners.

and the eastern one SWORD, was a five mile gap. Along this gap lay a number of small hamlets, and it was decided to clear the enemy out of these by landing two Commandos, 48 (Royal Marine) Commando at St. Aubin sur Mer, on the left hand edge of the 3rd (Canadian) Division on JUNO, and 41 (Royal Marine) Commando at Lion sur Mer on the left of the 3rd (British) Division on SWORD. These two Commandos would turn inwards and advance to meet each other, clearing the obstacles as they went and on

meeting link all British and Canadian Beaches into one continuous beachhead.

The story of 48 Commando on D-Day is a saga in itself.

48 (Royal Marine) Commando had been the last Commando raised for D-Day, and was formed from Marine Artillery units, and men of the 7th Battalion Royal Marines. The 7th Battalion had had a very chequered career in the Middle East, culminating in a very messy affair in Sicily, where, hastily reformed into an infantry unit, they had been put in to

attack a supposed weak Italian unit, which turned out to be some very aggressive elements of the German Herman Goring Division which gave the 7th Battalion a very bad time. They were returned to England in early 1944, reformed as a Commando, and given D-Day as their first operation.

Lt. Col. Moulton, their Commanding Officer, had been given various assurances about the landing but, being an experienced officer, made certain preparations of his own, just in case matters went wrong. In the event this proved to be a wise precaution.

48 Commando were to land at St. Aubin, two hours after the Canadians' first assault and presumably over quiet beaches, after which they would assemble, sort themselves out, and proceed calmly with their appointed task. However, when the Commando's craft arrived off the beaches, they noted that a considerable amount of firing seemed to be going on, and there seemed to be a lot of wreckage on shore. Orders were orders, however, and at the appointed time the Commando went in to land.

Their craft had reached the first line of half submerged obstacles, close enough to discover that the wreckage on the beach was craft, vehicles, equipment and men, still pinned down, when a storm of artillery fire broke over the oncoming craft.

88mm guns at point blank range wrought havoc among the landing craft, until the mortar men, whom Lt. Col. Moulton had prudently positioned in the bows of the L.S.I's were able to drop smoke bombs onto the beach thus screening their craft from direct fire. In this startling confusion the Commandos went ashore, wading through heavy seas, among wrecked and burning craft, and the dead and wounded bodies of the Canadians who were supposed to have cleared the beach two hours before. On the fire-swept beach, more shocks awaited the Commandos and not all the Commandos even got ashore. Some landing craft were sunk, and the strong tide carried the men away and drowned them. One troop, were rescued from their sinking craft by an L.S.T. The Captain of the L.S.T. had done his bit and put his tanks ashore, and was on his way back to England fast. The Commando troops, screaming and protesting were taken along as well. Some men, determined to land, threw off their equipment and dived overboard into the heavy seas to swim ashore, only to be drowned in the surf.

Lt. Col. Moulton reached the assembly area, which was found to be under mortar fire, to discover that his unit had lost all its machine guns, all but one mortar, and forty per cent of the troops, including one complete rifle troop, now being shipped reluctantly back to England. They had not yet fired a shot against the enemy. 'I begun to realise' said Col. Moulton later, 'that something very like disaster had overtaken 48 Commando.'

Nevertheless 48 (Royal Marine) Commando, like so many other units on D-Day, made the best of it, and set out to accomplish its task and after much fierce fighting and further casualties finally took the strong point at Langrune, until days later they met up with 41 (Royal Marine) Commando, coming from SWORD.

41 (Royal Marine) Commando had also had a bad landing, and soon ran into difficulty outside Lion-sur-Mer. At nightfall they were still held fast, when 21st Panzer pushed a prong of infantry and armour through to the coast at Luc-sur-Mer, cutting the invasion

German dead.

force in two. The German thrust luckily was too little and too late. It could not be supported and 21st Panzer were discouraged by the massed landings of the reserve units of 6th Airborne, and came under increasing pressure from 3rd (British) Division advancing from SWORD.

SWORD Beach lies at La Breche just to the west of Ouistreham at the outlet of the Caen Canal. From SWORD to Caen was nine miles. The German defences here were particularly intricate, and lay among a comparatively built up area. The houses in the villages of Riva Bella, La Breche and Lion had been turned into fortresses, while the low country behind had been flooded and mined. The beaches were also mined, heavily wired, studded with concrete emplacements and pillboxes, and protected offshore with the usual array of underwater obstacles. The Naval assembly areas were also in range of the heavy German guns across the Seine at Le Havre. This was the only assault area to experience attack by German Naval forces. Three E-boats attacked

Commandos press inland, past a bridge-laying tank.

Tanks of 3rd Infantry Division in trouble on the beach at Hermanville.

the Fleet with torpedos and sank the Norwegian destroyer 'Svenner'.

3rd (British) Division were instructed to secure the high ground North of Caen, and if possible Caen itself, and link up with 6th Airborne at Benouville and Ranville. 3rd Division Infantry were supported in the assault by D-D tanks of 13/18 Hussars, and Flails, Bulldozers and A.V.R.E's of the Royal Engineers. The tanks were engaged by the enemy the moment they touched the beach and only thirteen Shermans survived to give

cover for the infantry as they came ashore.

The assault companies came from the East Yorks., and South Lancashire Regiments and they suffered heavy casualties from the entrenched German infantry, in positions just across the dunes in the rear of SWORD Beach.

Obstacle clearance in the face of heavy and accurate fire proceeded only slowly, and at the expense of heavy casualties. The tide had kept most of the obstacles covered, and the gapping teams had to swim among the surf, cutting the mines and explosions free, to

British dead before the German defences.

make a passage for the 1st Suffolks who came ashore in one wave of twenty-five L.C.A's and were quickly in action.

By 9.00 a.m. 3rd (British) Division had cleared the enemy from La Breche and Hermanville, and were advancing inland towards Colleville on the banks of the Caen Canal. There remained the capture of Ouistreham.

This was the task of 4 Commando, reinforced for the occasion by two troops of French Commandos, under Commandant Phillipe Keiffer. Here, as elsewhere, the Commandos landed behind the assault infantry, only to discover a fire fight in progress on the beach, and their landing impeded by dead and wounded infantry and the wreckage from the assault waves. 4 Commando, and the French, circled Ouistreham from the west, and attacked the beach defences from the rear, the German strong point at the Casino being eliminated by the French troops. At 1400 hours, only two minutes late, Lord Lovat's piper led the rest

British infantry come ashore.

Canadian infantry at Bernieres.

124

Even horses get pressed into service.

of 1 Commando Brigade across the newly named Pegasus Bridge at Benouville, and linked up with the Airborne forces. With the capture of Ouistreham the sea landings were complete. For fifty miles along the coast, the enemy were under pressure, and being driven back by air attack, Naval gunfire and the advancing Allied Armies. There were gaps in this front of course, and some reverses. The Germans fought tenaciously for the ground and gave way only with the greatest reluctance. But Hitler's Atlantic Wall had no depth to it. Once breached at one point the rest of the defences could be outflanked and overwhelmed.

By mid-afternoon it was clear that the Battle of Normandy had started, for the Battle of D-Day had been won.

AFTERMATH

The Battle of Normandy, and the final destruction of Hitler's Germany, are outside the scope of this book. There exists a vast number of other works on that subject, and the interested reader must pursue his studies elsewhere.

It remains only to sum up the Battle of D-Day, and review the battlefield today.

On the evening of the Sixth of June, the Allies held a front of 50 miles along the Normandy coast, to a maximum depth of 7 miles. Bayeux fell on the following day, to troops of the 50th Northumbrian Division. Caen held out until the 10th July, and was totally destroyed in the fighting. On the American front, Carentan fell on 12th June, and Cherbourg on the 27th June. On the 18th July, after bitter fighting, the Americans took St. Lô.

The Battle of Normandy ended on 27th August. It cost the Allies over 200,000 men, including 36,000 dead. The German losses exceeded 300,000.

The D-Day casualties, killed, wounded and missing, did not exceed 10,000, which was wonderfully light for such an operation, and for such a gain.

The Normandy fighting also saw the end of Field Marshal Rommel. His staff car was strafed by Allied aircraft on 17th July, and while recovering from his injuries, suspected of complicity in the 20th July attempt on Hitler's life, he was forced to take poison and so died. Two Allied Commanders did not long survive the Battle. Admiral Ramsay and Air Chief Marshal Leigh Mallory were both killed in air crashes.

Eisenhower and Montgomery survived the war, and rose to the highest commands and honours their countries could bestow; Eisenhower eventually to become President of the United States.

Normandy today, a quarter of a century and more after the battle, bears few marks of the last and greatest land battle in history. When one considers that over two million men fought for three months across the province, it is remarkable how little permanent damage has resulted.

This is, in fact, something of an illusion,

A shattered German encasement on Juno Beach.

Overleaf: Abbey aux Dames, Caen.

Memorial to 13th (Lancashire) BN,
the Parachute Regiment, at Ranville.

and owes much to the practice of the French people, in restoring their shattered towns and villages to their former appearance, and avoiding the worst excesses of post-war architecture.

Both Caen and St. Lô were completely destroyed, but seem today to be old towns, with little indication that they were rebuilt from rubble within the last 25 years.

Along the D-Day beaches, there are many reminders and memorials of the Sixth of June.

In the East, across the Orne, where 6th Airborne landed, the empty casements of the Merville Battery still crouch in the fields above Franceville. Nearby, the bodies of the men who stormed the Battery, lie with those of other paratroops and commandos, in the British Cemetery at Ranville.

It is an easy march from here to Pegasus Bridge by the Caen Canal and it is still Pegasus

The Commando memorial, Ranville.

The 6th Royal Airborne Division landed near this bridge
on the night of 5th June 1944 as a Spearhead to the
Allied Armies of Liberation
La 6ème Division aéroportée Britannique a atterri à
Proximité de ce Pont dans la nuit du 5 au 6 Juin 1944
en tant que flèche des Armées alliées de Libération

Pegasus Bridge.

A D-D tank at Courseulles. This one was dredged from the sea in 1970.

The path of 48 Commando R.M., Langrune.

Now restored, this house overlooked Juno Beach.

The beach at St. Aubin.

Bridge, with large notice boards announcing the fact at either end. Examine the bridge closely, and the bullet holes and shrapnel scars still act as a reminder of the Sixth of June.

At Ouistreham, where 4 Commando and the Free French came ashore, there is an intriguing little museum by the Casino, and a memorial window to the Commandos in the Parish Church.

Along SWORD Beach, the guns are still there, rusting in their emplacements and slowly disappearing under the drifting sand. They dredged a D-D tank out of the sea off JUNO Beach twenty years after the war, and it now sits in the Square at Courseulles.

Courseulles and Bernaires contain plaques and memorials to Canadian Regiments while at Langrune, close by a 'Voie de 48 Commando' marks the path down which Colonel Moulton led his depleted unit to the battle.

The Invasion has an official remembrance at Arromanches, where the D-Day Museum displays a range of landing craft, weapons, maps and plans, while offshore, the pontoons and cassions of the British Mulberry still show above the sea.

At Port en Bessin, where the Allied Armies met, there is nothing to indicate that 47 (Royal Marine) Commando, once fought a battle there. It is again a small port, smelling strongly of fish.

SUR CETTE PLAGE DE
SAINT-AUBIN A L'AUBE
DU 6 JUIN 1944 A 7H30
FUT ETABLIE UNE TÊTE
DE PONT PAR LE RÉGIMENT
D'INFANTERIE CANADIENNE
DES "NORTH SHORE",
OUVRANT LA VOIE AU
48ème COMMANDO
DES "ROYAL MARINES"

Pages 134/135: *48 Commando landed here on D-Day.*

Above OMAHA Beach, the huge American Cemetery contains 9,000 graves, and an impressive memorial to the missing.

On the beach itself, the wreckage of the battle can still be found, in the jutting angle-iron of an old obstacle, or the sand filled outline of a wrecked landing craft.

The remains of an assault craft in the sands of Omaha.

The U.S. memorial above Omaha beach.

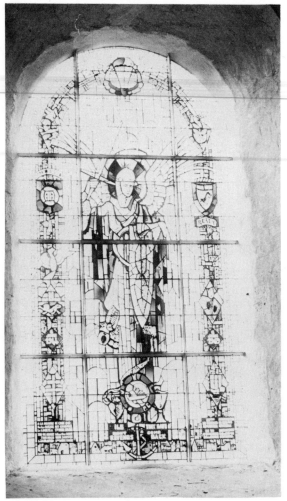

The window to the 82nd U.S. Airborne in the church at Ste-Mere-Eglise.

101st Airborne Museum at Carentan.

Visitors swarm on the Pointe du Hoc, where Colonel Rudder's Rangers once climbed with great difficulty, and the floods around Carentan have long drained back into their rivers.

The 101st Airborne have a museum here, with interesting relics, and a unique collection of German uniforms and equipment.

The American Airborne Museum at Ste-Mere-Eglise is well worth a visit, and the landings are also commemorated by a beautiful window in the fine Norman Church that dominates the great Square.

On UTAH, a few tanks and guns still commemorate the landings, while near La Fiere, a solitary foxhole marks where General James Gavin of the 82nd Airborne, fought for a while a very small scale war.

Inland, at Bayeux, it is the Tapestry of Bishop Odo, which attracts visitors to the town, and few seem to notice the plaque outside the Cathedral, commemorating another, later invasion, and the 50th Division, which freed Bayeux from the Germans.

The cemeteries, according to the registers, still receive plenty of visitors, mostly old soldiers, revisiting, as soldiers will, the sights of old campaigns, and remembering old friends and comrades left behind.

They have the satisfaction of knowing that their Battle was a decisive one, the final, definite nail in the coffin of Fortress Europe.

Four years after Dunkirk, the Allies landed again in France, and eleven months later, on 8th May, 1945, the War in Europe was over.

On the cliffs of Pointe du Hoc.

IN PROUD MEMORY
OF OUR DEAD

1ST ENGINEER
SPECIAL BRIGADE

H-HOUR 0630
D DAY 6 JUNE 1944

BIBLIOGRAPHY

The Battle of D-Day, William McElwee — Faber.

Dawn of D-Day, David Howarth — Collins.

Assault Division, N. Scarfe — Collins.

The Struggle for Europe, Chester Wilmott — Collins.

Path of the 50th, E. W. Clay — Gale & Polden.

The Sixth Airborne Division in Normandy, Sir Richard Gale.

A Soldier's Story, Gen. Omar Bradley — Eyre & Spotteswood.

Operation Neptune, Kenneth Edwards — Collins.

Omaha Beach to Cherbourg — Historical Division U.S. Army.

The Green Beret (The Commandos), Hilary St. George Saunders — Michael Joseph.

The Red Beret (The Parachute Regiment at War), Hilary St. George Saunders — Michael Joseph.

The War at Sea Vol. 3 Pts. II & III, Roskill — H.M.S.O.

The Mighty Endeavour.

The Battle for Normandy, Belfield & Essame — Batsford

The Second World War, Winston Churchill.

The Longest Day, Cornelius Ryan.

History of the 15th Scottish Division, H. G. Martin.

The Other Side of the Hill, Capt. Liddell Hart — Portway.

D. Day, R. W. Thompson — Pan/Ballentine.

With the Screaming Eagles on D. Day.

The Watery Maze, Bernard Fergusson.

Swiftly they Struck (4 Commando).

Haste to the Battle (48 Commando) Maj. Gen. J. L. Loulton.

The Assault Phase of the Normandy Landings, Admiral Ramsey.

Crusade in Europe, Dwight D. Eisenhower.

The War at Sea, Capt. Roskill.

The Airborne Museum, Aldershot, and museums at Carantan, Ste - Mere - Eglise, Arromanches, Cherbourg, Portsmouth, and H.M.S. Belfast, London, with The Imperial War Museum, are well worth a visit.

Photographs are reprinted and reproduced by permission of The Imperial War Museum, The Radio Times, Hulton Picture Library and various private sources, to all of whom the authors give thanks.

INDEX

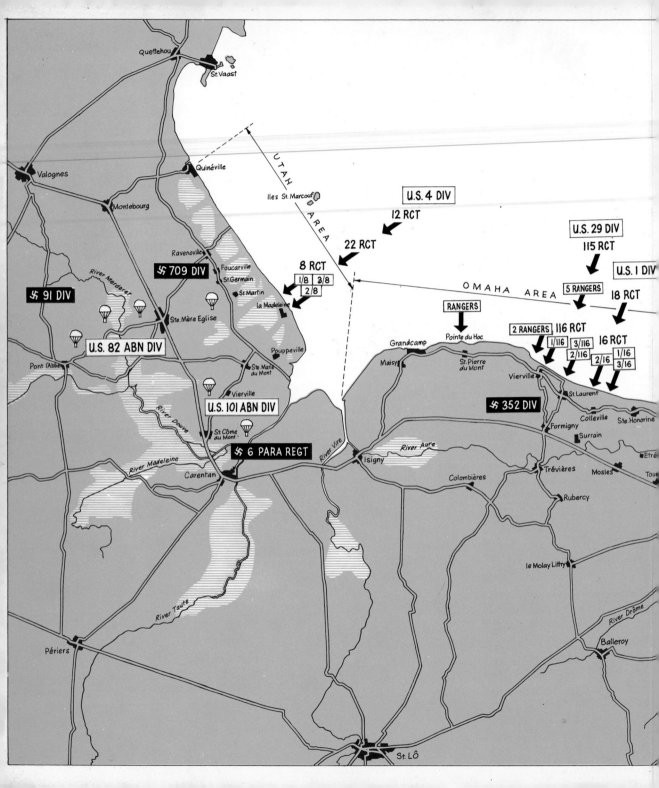